Religious Experience

Its Nature, Types and Validity

by

A. C. BOUQUET, D.D.

SECOND EDITION

Completely Revised

PHILLIPS MEMORIAL
LIBRARY
PROVIDENCE COLLEGE

GREENWOOD PRESS, PUBLISHERS
WESTPORT, CONNECTICUT

BL
53
B64
1976

Library of Congress Cataloging in Publication Data

Bouquet, Alan Coates, 1884-
    Religious experience : its nature, types, and
validity.

    Reprint of the ed. published by W. Heffer, Cambridge.
    Includes bibliographical references.
    1. Experience (Religion) 2. Psychology, Religious.
I. Title.
BL53.B64   1976   248'.2   75-40997
ISBN 0-8371-8714-1

© A. C. Bouquet, 1968

This edition originally published in 1968 by W. Heffer &
Sons Ltd., Cambridge

Reprinted with the permission of W. Heffer & Sons Ltd.

Reprinted in 1976 by Greenwood Press,
a division of Williamhouse-Regency Inc.

Library of Congress Catalog Card Number 75-40997

ISBN 0-8371-8714-1

Printed in the United States of America

RELIGIOUS EXPERIENCE

CONTENTS

* Reference to an Additional Footnote is made by a bold letter in the margin.

AUTHOR'S NOTE

The core of this book has been out of print for some time, but its contents have been found so useful when verbally reproduced at a college study-circle with which in the last eighteen months I have been working, that they seem to me to be relevant to the present religious situation. I have therefore asked my publishers to reissue them as a paperback, with a new introduction and tailpiece, some small revisions of the text, and a few additional footnotes which will be found at the end of the book.

I desire to acknowledge with gratitude the permission to make extracts from various original sources:

(1) To the Clarendon Press for permission to quote from Pope's translation of Tamil Hymns and McAuliffe's *The Sikh Religion*, and also from *Joseph Estlin Carpenter: a Memorial Volume* by C. H. Herford.

(2) To Messrs. Geo. Allen & Unwin for permission to quote from their translation of Heiler's *Gospel of Sadhu Sundar Singh*.

(3) To Messrs. Macmillan for permission to quote from Professor J. B. Pratt's *The Religious Consciousness*.

(4) To Messrs. Longmans, Green & Co. for permission to make extracts from William James's *Varieties of Religious Experience*.

October 1967   A. C. Bouquet

Wordsworth's famous sonnet is just as appropriate today as when it was first composed:

The world is too much with us; late and soon,
Getting and spending, we lay waste our powers:
Little we see in Nature that is ours;
We have given our hearts away, a sordid boon!

INTRODUCTION

It has always been possible for people to suffer an eclipse of memory where the Source of their being is concerned. Moses is thus represented in the book of Deuteronomy as saying to the Hebrew nation: "When thou hast eaten and art full, then beware lest thou forget the Lord thy God." In other words, affluence is one major condition which makes such forgetfulness extremely likely, and involves one in irresponsible behaviour and in lack of a sense of answerability to the Voice of Conscience within. In the earlier part of the nineteenth century when middle-class Britons were in the heyday of their prosperity, Tom Hughes wrote a continuation of his earlier work, which he called *Tom Brown at Oxford*, in the course of which he depicted some undergraduates as discussing the possibility of "belief in a dead God". It is therefore, I think, not altogether incongruous that under the conditions recently prevailing both in the United States and Great Britain we should be experiencing a recrudescence of this combination, and hear complaints of secularisation in both societies, of people trying to do without any form of religion, and living comfortably without God; and of siren voices on both sides of the Atlantic talking glibly about "the death of God". The latter may be nonsense, but it is certainly dangerous nonsense, and may be a contributory occasion for an epidemic of shallow teenage atheism, and also for the alarming decline in general moral standards and in responsible behaviour, especially in the stewardship of purchasing power, which I feel is likely to last for some time. Of course one must carefully distinguish between the death of an image of God[1] and the total disappearance of Deity, which would be an absurdity. Our actual image of the Latter must always be subject to growth, as it was in the case of the early Christians, who were sometimes branded by their contemporaries as atheists. But there is a finality about the basic Christian concept which is unlikely to suffer eclipse, although its expression may go on changing and developing. The six principles[2] which the Bishop of Woolwich indicates as characteristic of the more serious-minded of our younger generation seem to me to be derived from a recognition of the attributes of the God Within, Christianly conceived. It is significant that in the Fourth Gospel Jesus is represented as speaking of this development: "The Spirit will lead you into all truth. All things that the Father hath are mine: therefore said I that He (the Spirit) shall take of mine and shall show it unto you." And again: "Greater things shall he do (than Me), because I go to the Father; for my Father is greater than I." These are ideas which one hardly expects a disciple of Jesus to have invented, unless he was some unknown and unidentified genius. It seems most probable that we have here traditional

---

[1] The idea of the spatial transcendence of Deity, with a three-storied universe, seven heavens above, and a flat earth with hell underneath it, is of course as dead as a doornail.

[2] Integrity, justice, solidarity with and responsibility for one's fellow human beings, the value of the individual person for his or her own sake, and the quality of relationship as the ultimate test of right and wrong rather than some external rule. *But that I can't believe.* pp. 125–6).

logia which in spite of their context come from a non-synoptic source which goes back to Jesus Himself.

Scientific humanism may well be destructive of naïve fundamentalism. It certainly is. But it is ready to respect a liberal and intelligently based faith. Humanism itself gives no really satisfactory or adequate answer to those whose experiences I invite the reader here to examine, but it can be and often is used by the worldly and careless as an excuse of justification for their secularism.

It seems therefore worth while to review briefly the broad basis for the religious experiences of mankind. Only too often it has been supposed that this was not properly discoverable except through a study of the pages of the Bible, revealing what the late Hendrik Kraemer called "biblical realism". And yet I recall episodes in recent years when I was conscious that somebody with whom I had casually come into contact, and who did not belong to any Christian community, was just as much as any Catholic Christian in touch with the Great Basic Reality above, behind, and through life. Thus I remember travelling by train one night from Calcutta to Delhi in company with a Sikh who at dawn composed himself cross-legged on the carriage-seat opposite me, devoutly murmuring passages from the Japji; of a Hindu chairman at a college business meeting, who called upon a student to open the proceedings by reciting religious mantras from the Upanishads; of a hushed moment in a south Indian temple at evening sacrifice, when a small choir of children chanted in archaic Sanskrit a sentence which ran (in translation) "Thou art He Who is: Thou art the beginning and the ending"; and of a moment of silence in a North African mosque, when its custodian stood beside me in front of the tomb of a Muslim saint, fingering his rosary, and reciting softly with closed eyes "the beautiful names of God".

And so, in the pages which follow, I venture to ask my readers to consider once again the general basis for the intuitive awareness of Self-Existent Deity; for it is a human phenomenon shared by Christians with many who belong to very different religious backgrounds, and is a major factor in the production of wholeness and purposiveness of life. To let it fade, especially in what is to me most precious, the fullness of its Christian expression, will most certainly lead to the impoverishment of the human race, and rob it of any true sense of moral purpose. Thus for example the prevalence of the practices on a wide scale of betting and gambling may very largely be traced to the lack of a sense of steward-ship, and not solely to the craving for excitement and relief from the monotony of machine-minding, whether in office or factory. Bishop Westcott used to stress the duty of using one's purchasing power with the maximum of rationality and responsibility. But if the belief fades that there is an Ultimate Power to whom we are answerable for our spending (whether that Power be within or beyond us), it becomes only too easy to get into the way of believing that one can submit one's cash to the arbitrament of chance. And who cares?

It will be noticed that the examples I have chosen for illustration are from the confessions of a considerable variety of believers. While I deeply appreciate the sympathetic attitude of Sir Julian Huxley towards religion in his last volume of essays, I cannot feel that he has done justice to the significance of religious awareness both on its immanental side and in its sense of responsibility to a holy God. To take only one example, he seems to ignore the experiences of Quaker scientists such as Dr. Kathleen Lonsdale and Professor W. H. Thorpe. Nevertheless I feel bound to confess that just as between 800 B.C. and 300 A.D. (with perhaps isolated extensions on the fringe at either end) mankind as a whole, or at any rate in its more advanced areas of culture, passed through what Karl Jaspers has called the Axial Age, so mankind, since the Renaissance in Europe, and still more since the incorporation of the Royal Society in London in 1662, has drawn near to what may well be called "the second Axial Age", in which religion is not eliminated (that is impossible) but during which its outward expression is having to undergo more drastic changes than it has ever hitherto known. Like the first Axial Age, ours is one in which every institution, and not only religious ones, tend to be challenged. Thus in the sphere of law responsible people are asking why we should have coroners' courts, and are questioning the value of even the jury system. Change and renovation are everywhere in evidence.

Yet even such changes cannot destroy the fundamental relationship between the individual and that Self-Existent and Ultimate Being to Whom he owes his own finite existence, and within Whom he lives and moves with delegated spontaneity, however perversely and obstinately he may from time to time ignore the fact.

It is only fair however to recognise that the intuitional

experience of the Self-Existent Being comes along three broad lines, namely (to use the nomenclature of a Czech Jesuit of about forty years ago), Distance and Majesty; Depths of the Ego; and Stream of Process. Distance and Majesty of course does not mean spatial but qualitative transcendence, awe in the Presence of the morally Holy, a transcendence (as Dr. Nairne once put it) *within* the immanence, consciousness of one's utter finite imperfection, and of one's total obligation to be loyal to principle, even at the cost of one's life. It is a real and genuine experience, not to be regarded as limited to Hebrew prophetism or the pages of the Arabic Quran.[1]   Nevertheless a scrutiny of the examples I have chosen will show, I am confident, that the great bulk of God-consciousness is frankly immanental. Atheism is a misnomer except as denominating the rejection of a restricted and traditional theism, or of a naive conception of spatial transcendence such as lingers unfortunately in the wording of many hymns. In the wider sense, simply as the rejection of *any* concept of Self-Existent Being, hardly anyone (possibly no one) can be an atheist.   What matters of course is the kind of attribute with which the percipient invests

---

[1] The Jesuit in the foregoing quotation, Fr. Erich Przywara, went on to point out that a great deal of religious experience oscillates between these three main poles, thus comprising the many diverse religious experiences of mankind, non-Christian as well as Christian, naive as well as sophisticated.   He contended that only a true and enlightened Christian Catholicism is to be judged the proper repository of such varied experiences, holding all the various types and sub-types in balance and tension.   There is much to be said in favour of this conclusion, provided that such a Catholicism already exists.   But it may well be that it is still only on its way to realisation, the process having perhaps been speeded up by Vatican II.   The Great Church is still in the womb of the future.

the Self-Existent. Sir Julian Huxley is typical of those who are reluctant to describe the Latter as Personal; and yet even he hovers on the fringe, anxious to avoid the stigma of anthropomorphism, yet incapable of discarding the use of the words awe and adoration. It is not without significance that it is not only professing Christians who have seen in the Self-Existent a Being with whom it is possible to enter into relationship, Who is intelligent, Self-Limiting, and Benevolent, and Who both contains and pervades the universe. How well I remember dear old Baron von Hügel once saying to me as we walked beside his Pekinese in Kensington Gardens: "Ze obscuwity of may life to my leetle dog is much ze same as ze obscuwity of ze life of God to me." And yet to the dog the Baron was not impersonal.

I only regret that copyright restrictions preclude my adding extracts from the recently published meditations of the late lamented Mr. Dag Hammerskjöld.

In one analysis[1] of the elements of belief we find them subdivided into (1) the traditional, (2) the natural, (3) the moral, (4) the affective, and (5) the rational. Of these the middle three seem to be connected especially with intuition, though upon each of them the reason soon begins to exercise itself. Another writer[2] divides the elements of conviction into (1) the coercive, (2) the pragmatic, and (3) the reflective. Here it is the first element, that which forces itself upon one without

[1] R. H. Thouless, *Introduction to the Psychology of Religion* (Camb. Univ. Press.)

[2] H. H. Farmer, *Experience of God.*

immediate rational justification, which is connected with the intuitive faculty.

Intuitional experience plainly forms the material of what eighteenth-century writers called "revealed religion," though of course no one can seriously pretend that all alleged intuitions constitute genuine revelations, or that all such genuine revelations are of equal moment. At the same time it is curious to discover (as we certainly sometimes do) persons who deny that there is any knowledge of God which is capable of being derived from intuition, since the latter, they say, is only telescoped reasoning masquerading as a distinct source of information; and also persons who though they acknowledge that possibly some human beings may have or have had such intuitional experiences, yet deny that they have ever had any themselves.[1]

Catholic apologists, though rejecting a primary appeal to experience, allow the argument from conscience and from universal consent as among other proofs, and accept, after careful analysis, the evidence of private revelations, but they object that to rely chiefly on intuitional data is to reduce Deity to a mere aspect of religious emotion, and to substitute a vague affective feeling for that which can be the object of cognition as well. The importance of avoiding this danger, and of maintaining balance and proportion between the two sides of the argument is admittedly not negligible, yet it can hardly be denied that the modern emphasis upon direct experience has enormously strengthened the

[1] To the former class should certainly be assigned the late Dr. F. R. Tennant and the late Dean Rashdall, and to the latter (in spite of his famous Gifford Lectures) the late Professor William James.

position of religion. Indeed it may well be said that to approach an unbeliever merely with the arguments from reason will have little effect upon him, unless we also how him that there is well-attested evidence showing that many human beings of undoubted sanity have experienced friendship with a Being corresponding to the One the probability of whose existence has previously been indicated, and that such friendship has borne positive and beneficial fruits.

An Anglican philosopher[1] has drawn a pleasing comparison between the homing pigeon and the navigation officer. The pigeon has no knowledge of nautical mathematics, but it gets home all the same. The navigation officer, by a rather more laborious process of calculation, works out the course of his ship and brings her into port. He is slower than the pigeon, but on the other hand his intelligence and general capacity for creative 'action are greater than those of the bird. We see a somewhat similar situation in the sphere of religion. A simple peasant with very limited powers of reasoning and reflection may as an untutored mystic arrive at a vision of reality more quickly than the scientific theologian. Nevertheless it would be unjust to rate the work of the one as either more or less valuable than the work of the other. Their functions in life are different, and each has need of the other's experience. In this volume we propose to consider the experience of the believer, whose perception of Deity comes either from the sense of presence in nature, in the course of events or in the inner life. This is not quite

---

[1] The late Professor O. C. Quick.

the same as the argument from universal consent, but it is rather an argument from the universal consent of experts, concerning whom it has been well pointed out that the approach which they make is much the same, whatever their religious beliefs; so that it is difficult to say without reference to the context whether a mystical passage is taken from the writings of a Christian, Indian or Moslem. "In reading extracts from the great mystics we might often be in doubt whether the writer was a Neo-Platonist, a Sufi, a Buddhist, a Catholic, or a Quaker. Mysticism is pure religion, and for this reason the great Churches have never been able to do without it, and yet have never been able to control it entirely, or subordinate it to their aims."[1]

It has sometimes been said, however, that the eastern mystics differ profoundly from the western in the nature of the goal which they propose for the human spirit. Both begin with a direct perception of a strength and vivacity which takes them by storm. Both experience times of rapture and coldness and both develop the practice of spiritual exercises for the purpose of inducing and strengthening the states of consciousness in which they delight. The easterns, however, with some exceptions, are said to aim, not merely at a harmony with the divine Being in which the separate

---

[1] Inge, *Christian Ethics*, p. 121. But Dr. Oman (appendix to *The Natural and the Supernatural*) commends to us a different view of the facts, and draws an important distinction between natural or unorganised mysticism and mysticism which if not organised, is at least artificially induced by the exercises referred to above. (For a comparative account of the latter, see A. Tillyard, *Spiritual Exercises*.)

existence of the individual soul is preserved, but at
complete annihilation of the self, which is thus totally
absorbed in Deity.   The westerns on the other hand,
stop short at the point of complete harmony, sometimes
compared to spiritual marriage, because in human
marriage the man and the woman, though they become
one flesh, are still twain.   It is very difficult to be quite
sure that in making this distinction one is doing justice
to both groups.   While on the one hand the language of
the orientals seems unmistakable, at the same time we
need to remember that it is the poetical language of
ecstasy, and that although much of it may be set in a
pantheistic background, even this pantheism may not
always be meant to be taken literally.   The following
quotation, although translated from a Moslem (Sufi)
poet, might easily have been written by Charles
Wesley, and does not necessarily involve the total
annihilation of the self:

> With Thy Sweet Soul, this soul of mine
> Hath mixed as Water doth with Wine.
> Who can the Wine and Water part,
> Or me and Thee when we combine?
> Thou art become my greater self;
> Small bounds no more can me confine.
> Thou hast my being taken on,
> And shall not I now take on Thine?
> Me thou for ever hast affirmed,
> That I may ever know Thee mine.
> Thy Love has pierced me through and through,
> Its thrill with Bone and Nerve entwine.
> I rest a Flute laid on Thy lips;
> A lute, I on Thy breast recline.

Breathe deep in me that I may sigh;
Yet strike my strings, and tears shall shine.[1]

At the same time there does seem to be a marked difference between the pantheism of some of the Upanishads, in which the many are completely whelmed and lost in the one, and the pantheism of western mystics, which endeavours to keep the many within the one.

I have added opposite, to preface this new edition, Emily Brontë's famous poem which, after having remained unnoticed by many in recent years, now seems as though it may become the marching song of immanental (I won't say "Robinsonian") theology. It should be borne in mind that Emily came of Irish stock: her poem—although the rhapsodical utterance of the daughter of an Anglican parson—has something of the Celtic fervour which one associates with W. B. Yeats.

---

[1] Compare Cowper, translating Mme. Guyon:

O Glory, in which I am lost,
    Too deep for the plummet of thought
On an ocean of Deity tossed,
    I am swallowed, I sink into naught.

and also: "My *me* is God, nor do I know my selfhood save in Him."

(St. Catherine of Genoa.)

No coward soul is mine,
No trembler in the world's storm-troubled sphere:
  I see Heaven's glories shine,
And faith shines equal, arming me from fear.

O God within my breast,
Almighty! ever-present Deity!
  Life—that in me has rest,
As I—undying Life—have power in Thee!

Vain are the thousand creeds
That move men's hearts: unutterably vain;
  Worthless as withered weeds,
Or idlest froth amid the boundless main,

To waken doubt in one
Holding so fast by Thine infinity;
  So surely anchored on
The steadfast rock of immortality.

With wide-embracing love
Thy Spirit animates eternal years,
  Pervades and broods above,
Changes, sustains, dissolves, creates, and rears.

Though earth and man were gone,
And suns and universes ceased to be,
  And Thou wert left alone,
Every existence would exist in Thee.

There is not room for Death,
Nor atom that his might could render void:
  Thou—THOU art Being and Breath,
And what THOU art may never be destroy'd.

MATERIALS

We will begin our survey with a few standard instances of experience, drawn partly from the well-known manuscript collections of Starbuck[1] and James,[2] but from other sources as well.

The first is that of an individual of no church connections of any kind, and is all the more impressive in sincerity because of the negative conclusion.

"Between twenty and thirty I gradually became more and more agnostic and irreligious, yet I cannot say that I ever lost that 'indefinite consciousness' which Herbert Spencer describes so well, of an Absolute Reality behind phenomena. For me this Reality was not the pure Unknowable of Spencer's philosophy, for although I had ceased my childish prayers to God, and never prayed to It in a formal manner, yet my more recent experience shows me to have been in a relation to It which practically was the same thing as prayer. Whenever I had any trouble, especially when I had conflict with other people, either domestically or in the way of business, or when I was depressed in spirits or anxious about affairs, I now recognise that I used to fall back for support upon this curious relation I felt myself to be in to this fundamental cosmical It. It was on my side, or I was on Its side, however you please to term it, in the particular trouble, and It always strengthened me and seemed to give me endless vitality to feel Its underlying and supporting presence. In fact, It was an unfailing fountain of living

[1] *Psychology of Religion.*
[2] *Varieties of Religious Experience.*

justice, truth, and strength, to which I instinctively turned
at time of weakness, and It always brought me out. I
know now that it was a personal relation I was in to It,
because of late years the power of communicating with It
has left me, and I am conscious of a perfectly definite loss.
I used never to fail to find It when I turned to It. Then
came a set of years when sometimes I found It, and then
again I would be wholly unable to make connection with It.
I remember many occasions on which at night in bed
I would be unable to get to sleep on account of worry.
I turned this way and that in the darkness, and groped
mentally for the familiar sense of that higher mind of my
mind which had always seemed to be close at hand as it
were, closing the passage, and yielding support, but there
was no electric current. A blank was there instead of It:
I couldn't find anything. Now, at the age of nearly
fifty, my power of getting into connection with It has
entirely left me; and I have to confess that a great help
has gone out of my life. Life has become curiously dead
and indifferent; and I can now see that my old experience
was probably exactly the same thing as the prayers of the
orthodox, only I did not call them by that name. What
I have spoken of as 'It' was practically not Spencer's
Unknowable, but just my own instinctive and individual
God, whom I relied upon for higher sympathy, but whom
somehow I have lost."

2. "I remember the night, and almost the very spot on
the hilltop, where my soul opened out, as it were, into the
Infinite, and there was a rushing together of the two worlds,
the inner and the outer. It was deep calling into deep,
—the deep that my own struggle had opened up within
being answered by the unfathomable deep without,
reaching beyond the stars. I stood alone with Him who
had made me, and all the beauty of the world, and love,
and sorrow, and even temptation. I did not seek Him,

but felt the perfect unison of my spirit with His. The ordinary sense of things around me faded. For the moment nothing but an ineffable joy and exaltation remained. It is impossible fully to describe the experience. It was like the effect of some great orchestra when all the separate notes have melted into one swelling harmony that leaves the listener conscious of nothing save that his soul is being wafted upwards, and almost bursting with its own emotion. The perfect stillness of the night was thrilled by a more solemn silence. The darkness held a presence that was all the more felt because it was not seen. I could not any more have doubted that He was there than that I was. Indeed, I felt myself to be, if possible, the less real of the two. . . .

. . . "My highest faith in God and truest idea of him were then born in me. I have stood upon the Mount of Vision since, and felt the Eternal round about me. But never since has there come quite the same stirring of the heart. Then, if ever, I believe, I stood face to face with God, and was born anew of his spirit. There was, as I recall it, no sudden change of thought or of belief, except that my early crude conception had, as it were, burst into flower. There was no destruction of the old, but a rapid, wonderful unfolding. Since that time no discussion that I have heard of the proofs of God's existence has been able to shake my faith. Having once felt the presence of God's spirit, I have never lost it again for long. My most assuring evidence of His existence is deeply rooted in that hour of vision, in the memory of that supreme experience, and in the conviction, gained from reading and reflection, that something the same has come to all who have found God. I am aware that it may justly be called mystical. I am not enough acquainted with philosophy to defend it from that or any other charge. I feel that in writing of it I have overlaid it with words rather than put it clearly to your thought. But, such as it is, I have described it as carefully as I now am able to do."

3. "I have on a number of occasions felt that I had enjoyed a period of intimate communion with the divine. These meetings came unasked and unexpected, and seemed to consist merely in the temporary obliteration of the conventionalities which usually surround and cover my life. . . . Once it was when from the summit of a high mountain I looked over a gashed and corrugated landscape extending to a long convex of ocean that ascended to the horizon, and again from the same point when I could see nothing beneath me but a boundless expanse of white cloud, on the blown surface of which a few high peaks, including the one I was on, seemed plunging about as if they were dragging their anchors. What I felt on these occasions was a temporary loss of my own identity, accompanied by an illumination which revealed to me a deeper significance than I had been wont to attach to life. It is in this that I find my justification for saying that I have enjoyed communication with God. Of course the absence of such a being as this would be chaos. I cannot conceive of life without its presence."

4. "God is more real to me than any thought or thing or person. I feel his presence positively, and the more as I live in closer harmony with his laws as written in my body and mind. I feel him in the sunshine or rain; and awe mingled with a delicious restfulness most nearly describes my feelings. I talk to him as to a companion in prayer and praise, and our communion is delightful. He answers me again and again, often in words so clearly spoken that it seems my outer ear must have carried the tone, but generally in strong mental impressions. Usually a text of Scripture, unfolding some new view of him and his love for me, and care for my safety. I could give hundreds of instances, in school matters, social problems,

financial difficulties, etc. That he is mine and I am his
never leaves me, it is an abiding joy. Without it life would
be a blank, a desert, a shoreless, trackless waste."

5. "God is quite real to me. I talk to him and often
get answers. Thoughts sudden and distinct from any I
have been entertaining come to my mind after asking God
for his direction. Something over a year ago I was for
some weeks in the direct perplexity. When the trouble
first appeared before me I was dazed, but before long
(two or three hours) I could hear distinctly a passage of
Scripture: 'My grace is sufficient for thee.' Every time
my thoughts turned to the trouble I could hear this quotation. I don't think I ever doubted the existence of God,
or had him drop out of my consciousness. God has
frequently stepped into my affairs very perceptibly, and
I feel that he directs many little details all the time. But
on two or three occasions he has ordered ways for me
very contrary to my ambitions and plans."

6. "Sometimes, as I go to church, I sit down, join in the
service, and before I go out I feel as if God was with me,
right side of me, singing and reading the Psalms with
me. . . . And then again I feel as if I could sit beside
him, and put my arms around him, kiss him, etc. When
I am taking Holy Communion at the altar, I try to get
with him and generally feel his presence."

7. "God surrounds me like the physical atmosphere.
He is closer to me than my own breath. In him literally
I live and move and have my being. . . . There are times
when I seem to stand in his very presence, to talk with
him. Answers to prayer have come, sometimes direct
and overwhelming in their revelation of his presence and
powers. There are times when God seems far off, but this
is always my own fault. . . . . I have the sense of a presence
strong, and at the same time soothing, which hovers over

me. Sometimes it seems to enwrap me with sustaining arms."

The following is the experience of a distinguished British scholar of recent times.

"I was in a condition of religious apathy for a long time when I was at M.N.C. I had no intellectual doubts: I do not think I am able to enter into them: that means perhaps that I had not widely departed from the philosophy in which I was trained. But though I had no doubts, I had no religion. I had no sense of personal relationship to God. I thought that I ought to leave the college, for services were a weariness to me. I never wished particularly to pray. I hoped that if I went for a time to work in some way among the poor and the ignorant, my religion might in some way be renewed in me. It was brought about, but not in that way. Dr. M. persuaded me to wait in the College, and one summer I went to stay with W. at his father's house in North Wales. Shall I tell you what happened to me? Well, I shall not see you smile, and I have no secrets from you. You know how to respect confidences. I went out one afternoon for a walk alone. I was in the empty unthinking state in which one saunters along country lanes, simply yielding oneself to the casual sights around which give a town-bred lad with country yearnings such intense delight. Suddenly I became conscious of the presence of someone else. I cannot describe it, but I felt that I had as direct a perception of the being of God all round about me as I have of you when we are together. It was no longer a matter of inference, it was an immediate act of spiritual (or whatever adjective you like to employ) apprehension. It came unsought, absolutely unexpectedly. I remember the wonderful transfiguration of the far-off woods and hills as they seemed to blend in the infinite Being with which I was thus brought into relation. This experience did

not last long. But it sufficed to change all my feeling.
I had not found God because I had never looked for him.
But he had found me; he had, I could not but believe,
made himself personally known to me. I had not gone
in search of a satisfying emotion, I did not work myself
up into this state by any artificial means. But I felt
that God had come to me, I could now not only believe in
him with my mind, but love him with my heart. I cannot
tell you how often this has come back to me both with
thankfulness and with humiliation. . . . I am often per-
plexed to know why such revealings do not come to other
souls. But I cannot regard this as a mere piece of roman-
ticism, though I shall not be surprised or offended if you
do. This event has never happened to me again. . . .
It was not necessary. The sense of a direct relation to
God then generated in my soul has become a part of my
habitual thought and feeling."[1]

We will now pass to some extracts from eastern
mystics, both Christian and non-Christian:—

The first two shall be drawn quite indiscriminately
from Indian non-Christian sources:—[1]

"All space is Thine, O Thou far and near, immanent
    Thou art,
And Thou well'st up as a living fountain of bliss in my
    heart."

          (Swami Tayumanavar—18th cent. A.D.)

"I know Thee, I lowest of men that live,
    I know and see myself a very cur,
    Yet, Lord, I'll say I am Thy loving one!
    Tho' such I was, Thou took'st me for Thine own!
    The wonder this! Say is there aught like this?
    He made me servant of his loving saint;
    Dispelled my fear; ambrosia pouring forth, He came,

[1] *Joseph Estlin Carpenter: a Memorial Volume*, by C. H. Herford.

And while my soul dissolved in love made me His own.
Henceforth I'm no one's vassal; none I fear,
>We've reached the goal!
(Manikka Vaçagar[1]—9th cent. A.D. Transl. G. V. Pope, Oxford, 1910.)

The third is from Kabir, the leader much revered by Sikhs:—

"Behold what wonderful rest is in the Supreme Spirit!
>and he enjoys it who makes himself meet for it.
Held by the cords of love, the swing of the ocean of joy sways to and fro; and a mighty sound breaks forth in song.
Music is all around it, and there the heart partakes of the joy of the Infinite Sea.
There the unstruck music is sounded; it is the music of the love of the Three Worlds.
Look upon life and death; there is no separation between them."
>(Kabir[2]—late 15th cent. A.D.)

The fourth is a Hebrew expression of this mystical sense of reality; that priceless treasure, the first eighteen verses of the 139th Psalm:—

O LORD, thou hast searched me, and known me.
Thous knowest my downsitting and mine uprising.
Thou understandest my thought afar off.
Thou searchest out my path and my lying down,
And art acquainted with all my ways.
For there is not a word in my tongue,
But, lo, O LORD, thou knowest it altogether.
Thou hast beset me behind and before.
And laid thine hand upon me.
Such knowledge is too wonderful for me;

[1] Quoted by J. Estlin Carpenter, *Indian Theism*.
[2] From McAuliffe, *The Sikh Religion*.

It is high, I cannot attain unto it.
Whither shall I go from thy spirit?
Or whither shall I flee from thy presence?
If I ascend up into heaven, thou art there:
If I make my bed in Sheol, behold, thou art there.
If I take the wings of the morning,
And dwell in the uttermost parts of the sea;
Even there shall thy hand lead me,
And thy right hand shall hold me.
If I say, Surely the darkness shall overwhelm me,
And the light about me shall be night;
Even the darkness hideth not from thee.
But the night shineth as the day;
The darkness and the light are both alike to thee.
For thou hast possessed my reins:
Thou hast covered me in my mother's womb.
I will give thanks unto thee; for I am fearfully and wonder-
    fully made:
Wonderful are thy works:
And that my soul knoweth right well.
When I was made in secret,
And curiously wrought in the lowest parts of the earth.
Thine eyes did see mine unperfect substance.
And in thy book were all my members written,
Which day by day were fashioned.
When as yet there was none of them.
How precious also are thy thoughts unto me, O God!
How great is the sum of them!
If I should count them, they are more in number than the
    sand:
When I awake, I am still with thee.

The fifth is from a Moslem mystic:—

Regard now what is this that lingers not
Before thine eye and in a moment fades.

All thou beholdest is the act of one
In solitude, but closely veiled is He.
Let Him but lift the screen, no doubt remains:
The forms are vanished, He alone is all;
And thou, illumined, knowest that by His light
Thou findest his actions in the senses' night.

(Ibnu 'l Larid—a sufi.)

We will add a few passages from the Gospel of Sadhu Sundar Singh, illustrating the experiences of a Christian oriental mystic of the present century.

This remarkable man (so it is believed) in the end sacrificed his life somewhere in the interior of Tibet for the cause to which he has devoted himself for many years past.

I. "We cannot live a single hour, without God. 'In Him we live and move and have our being.' But most of us are like people who are asleep, who breathe without being conscious of it. If there were no air round them, and they ceased to breathe, they would be neither asleep nor awake—they would die of suffocation. As a rule, however, men never think about the absolutely indispensable gift of the air we breathe. But if we do reflect upon it we are filled with thankfulness and joy. Our spiritual dependence upon God is something very like. that. He sustains us: we live in Him. Yet how many of us ever think about it? How many souls there are who really wake from slumber and begin to breathe in the Divine air, without which, if it were to be withdrawn, the soul would die of suffocation! What kind of breathing, then, is this? The breath of the soul is prayer, through which fresh currents of air sweep into our being, bringing with them fresh supplies of vital force from the Love of God, on whom our whole life depends. . . . All life comes from God, but most people never think about this at all; they are quite unconscious of their spiritual life. It is only when a man begins to pray that he becomes conscious of this relationship. Then he begins to think, and realises how wonderful it is to live in God."

2. "The wonderful peace which the man of prayer feels during his prayer is not the fruit of his own imagination or of his own thoughts, but it is the result of the Presence of God in his soul. The mist which rises from a pond cannot form itself into great clouds and return to the earth as rain. Great clouds can only be drawn up from the mighty ocean, and it is the rain which comes from them which refreshes and quickens the thirsty earth. Peace does not come from our subconscious life, but from the infinite ocean of the Love of God, with Whom we are united in prayer."

3. "I was talking once with a very learned man, a psychologist, who assured me that the wonderful peace which I experienced was simply the effect of my own imagination. Before I answered him I told him the story of a person who was blind from birth, and who did not believe in the existence of the sun. One cold winter day he sat outside in the sunshine, and then his friends asked him: 'How do you feel now?' He replied: 'I feel very warm.' 'It is the sun which is making you warm; although you cannot see it, you feel its effects.' 'No,' he said, 'that is impossible; this warmth comes from my own body; it is due to the circulation of the blood. You will never make me believe that a ball of fire is suspended in the midst of the heavens without any pillar to support it.' Well, I said to the psychologist, 'What do you think of the blind man?' 'He was a fool!' he answered. 'And you,' I said to him, 'are a learned fool!' You say that my peace is the effect of my own imagination, but *I* have experienced it'."

And we may add here the triumphant confession of George Fox the English seeker:—

"Now was I come up in spirit through the flaming sword, into the paradise of God. All things were new; and all the creation gave unto me another smell than before, beyond what words can alter. I know nothing but pureness, and innocency, and righteousness. . . . Great things did the Lord lead me into, and wonderful depths were opened unto me, beyond what can by words be declared; but as people come by subjection to the Spirit of God, and grow up in the image and power of the Almighty, they may receive the Word of Wisdom that opens all things, and come to know the hidden unity in the Eternal Being."

To these extracts we may finally add the striking confession of a French agnostic, quoted by Flournoy; all the more extraordinary as coming from one who had, for the time at any rate, become uncertain as to the validity of any dogmatic belief.

"I seem to feel within the depths of my being an action, a presence; in short I seem to be the object, even prior to being the subject, of an action that is spiritual. This is in part a rudimentary, half-conscious belief, in part it is simply the expression of a fact, the testimony to a sort of profound and vague sensation. I tell myself that this sensation may itself be an illusion, that there may be nothing real about it apart from my subjectivity; but it *is*, and that is enough for me to live by. . . . It is a part of my being and has for the rest of my being an importance and a value that are supreme—that suffices me. And for the rest, I tell myself that the very fact that I possess this experience called 'religious,' is a witness in me to the existence of the inaccessible reality; of the union within my consciousness of the me and the not-me; that in it I have in some measure an immediate knowledge of the roots of my being, of a bond between me and something else, this 'something else' being necessarily self-conscious since it passes within my self-consciousness. . . . And just because I have become agnostic, and because every intellectual formulation of the inaccessible is for me simply a representation of the Reality, without any value in itself, I feel myself on solid ground. I have the experience there within that I have not to act but to receive; that I have not the initiative but the duty of waiting and listening; that the source of life is beyond the conscious self, for me, for all men."[1]

ANALYSIS

It would be possible of course to multiply confessions of this kind almost indefinitely, but the ones I have given must suffice. It needs to be remembered that such records of experience require to be cautiously received. There is a certain type of decadent who is only too ready to open his neurotic mind to the public, and it does not follow that the individual who is most willing to answer a psychologist's questionnaire or write an autobiographical sketch is just the person who has had the richest and deepest experience. Others who have declined to unlock their secrets may have actually had a fuller perception of reality. Moreover, the intuitional experiences of the prophet, the seer, and the mystic need to be co-ordinated by comparison with the other types of evidence, and are accordingly guaranteed or invalidated by their discordance or harmony with the remainder of the data available. They must in fact pass the test of coherence. The

[1] The English translation is given in Prof. Pratt, *The Religious Consciousness*, page 474.

sanity and practicality of some intuitionists must not blind us to the existence of others who can only be described as pathological specimens.

The analysis of what is called religious consciousness has so often been undertaken in a spirit of callousness bordering upon irreverence that one trembles at the prospect of falling into the same error. One thing is certain, we can never hope to understand the data of religious experience merely by studying religious psychology, any more than we can understand the meaning of the musician's composition by a mere study of the method of writing a score or of the construction or working of musical instruments, or even the technique of playing upon them. It is necessary, therefore, to remind the reader that no one can hope to understand religion who does not live in the spirit of a worshipper. This is only another way of expressing the meaning of the renowned beatitude: "Blessed are the pure in heart, for they shall see God."

To see the meaning of the whole of existence is certainly not granted equally as a right to all human beings. Doubtless the power to win it is given to all, but not the thing itself, and we can hardly deny that in the rich variety of human types there are some who are naturally endowed with the power to win the vision more than others, even though they may waste or lose this power. Now the development and success of the faculty of seeing into the heart of reality depends above all else upon purity of motive. Probably no one has ever succeeded in expressing this better or more concisely than Mrs. Browning in her now almost commonplace passage from "Aurora Leigh":

"Earth's crammed with heaven,
And every common bush afire with God:
But only he who sees, takes off his shoes;
The rest sit round it and pluck blackberries."

As this stands it might seem to be a false antithesis, since some of us know that it is possible to pluck blackberries and to see earth crammed with heaven at the same time; but the poetess was doubtless thinking of those who stop short at the picking. He who is not pure in heart and who has no intention of being a worshipper will not be able to understand the experience of others or to have any satisfying experiences himself.

But it may be said: "Is not this an attempt to make everyone into a mystic, and is it not true that a large number of persons are incapable of becoming mystics to any great extent, but only of living quite decent and moral lives upon a humdrum level?" To the above objection the following reply may be offered: In so far as different persons are by nature differently endowed with the capacity for winning close contacts with reality we can agree that some will find it harder than others. It seems, however, that the objection that has been raised betrays a misunderstanding as to the nature of what is called mysticism, a misunderstanding which is really excusable. Mysticism undoubtedly means the immediate contact which is implied in being μύστης or initiate. But there is more than one avenue of approach to the state of being μύστης. It may be approached, as it is by a certain number, along the lines of an institution with sacramental rites. But it may also be approached by quietism, or along the lines of the sacramentalism of ordinary life, or by means of an organised process of self-hypnotism, leading to a state resembling unconsciousness or trance, and in every instance the initiation is into something different, not necessarily the truth in all cases. Mysticism may also manifest itself with many and varying degrees of intensity, and in a mild form it is almost universal.

When a certain bishop once asserted that the religion of the lorry-driver must be his lorry, he was saying something which was capable of several interpretations. The religion of the lorry-driver may be taken to mean either (1) a kind of bored acquiescence in having to mind and drive a machine, or (2) an acceptance of the duty of minding and driving a machine as part of the scheme of the universe, a little part it is true, yet somehow linked up with the entire programme.

In the case of (1) the machine is the limit of the driver's relationship and so it becomes in certain cases his deity, and a poor one at that. If he is really very much bored with it, he may even fail to get as far as giving it that amount of attention which is due to it. On the other hand, in the case of (2) the mechanic will engage in his task with pride and zest because he will see the care of his machine in a kind of cosmic setting.

On this very point strong modern testimony comes from a learned Oxford moralist:—

"So far then from being rare, the mystical experience is at once the commonest and the greatest of human accidents. There is not one of us to whom it does not come daily. It is only carelessness or custom that prevents our realising how divine it is in essence; only timidity which checks us from proclaiming that we too at such moments have seen God, even as in a glass darkly; only folly which blinds us to the fact that these moments of vision are our surest safeguard and our best resource in every temptation, sorrow, or selfishness. In every such contact with whatever is true and honourable and just and pure and lovely and of good report the true Christian tradition allows, and indeed constrains, us to recognise the first trace of the vision of God. What Christianity offers, with its fellowship and Sacraments, its life of prayer and service, its preaching of the Incarnate Son of God, is the same vision in ever-increasing plenitude; vouchsafed in such measure as will avail against the worst temptations, the deepest sorrows, the most ingrained self-seeking, and will give constant and daily increase of strength, encouragement and illumination."[1]

Now it may be admitted that the latter attitude is not altogether easy to acquire, but I do not feel convinced that it is harder to acquire than the profitable participation in a liturgical service: and since the latter occupies a very small fraction of the whole life of the average mortal (even if devout) compared with the time he spends at his steering wheel or at his sport, it is surely rather important that he should be encouraged to make himself μύστης under the latter conditions. It must be admitted that in the main the teachers of religion have devoted far less attention to it than they have to the business of trying to train people to be μύσται as the result of some liturgical exercise. The result is that many persons have

[1] K. Kirk, *The Vision of God* (Bampton Lectures, 1928).

developed independently, and I think quite justifiably, a mild mystical attitude of their own in relation to their work, and have perhaps been more successful in doing so than if their friends and pastors had helped them in that direction.

We revert then to the preliminary statement that without single-mindedness and the spirit of reverence there can be no hopeful approach to a vision of reality. We may argue about it and pick it to pieces and see bits of it, but we cannot see it as a whole either in others or in ourselves, unless we school ourselves to love and pursue the values which it embodies.

With these preliminary precautions in our minds we can now go on to examine our data.

It is the fashion to-day to speak of the religious consciousness as the alignment of the total number of human faculties upon the most important element in man's environment and to say that man is a religious animal, or, more correctly, is capable of becoming a religious animal. Attention is concentrated by psychologists upon the expression of the religious emotions, the reason, and the will, as testifying to the felt presence of the Divine. Man is able to establish contact and relationship with point after point in his environment, and in that environment the highest point is said to be Deity.

"Man," it has been said, "is placed in a real environment, not in an imaginary one. If there was no Being in man's environment to which the conception of Deity in some measure corresponded, man would not best succeed in adjusting himself to his environment by belief in Deity. Such a belief as this would be entirely quixotic in its effects . . . but the opposite is the fact, therefore Deity exists."[1]

And again the late Mr. Bernard Bosanquet says:—

"The instinctive appetite or demand for Deity is a proof of the reality of Deity in the same sort of sense in which hunger is a proof of the existence of food, or the sexual impulse proof of the existence of possible mates. Of course obvious exceptions take place: you may starve; you may die unmated. But *in rerum natura* an instinct implies an object; and if you find a special emotional impulse, such as that of worship and religion, which pervades all sorts of particular experiences, but maintains its unique suggestions and demands throughout them all, you can hardly help recognising the object of this emotion as at least some peculiar feature of the world."[2]

1. *Source and Origin*

What are the *source and origin* of the intuitional religious experience? On this matter it seems best to state the facts clearly and frankly, and to admit at once, what it is difficult to deny, that that experience has its fountain-head in the biological realm of the individual. So for the matter of that have the creative achievements of art and literature. Man is made with a certain raw element within him, known to the psychologists as "libido." This is like a stream which can be dammed up and controlled and made serviceable for a variety of purposes. If left to run

---

[1] W. K. Wright, *A Student's Philosophy of Religion*, 1922.
[2] In *Contemporary Philosophy* (1921), p. 67.

unchecked, it expresses itself incontinently in the pursuit of sex-experiences. If controlled, *i.e.* repressed from the sex-direction and re-directed or sublimated, it can be the source of a variety of creative operations, in which knowledge is acquired and expressed. One of these is the numinous experience, in which the knowledge of God is acquired and expressed. Such an experience is a real sublimation of human personality and the divine. There is both giving and receiving on both sides, and the human being records a certain sense of fatigue after the intercourse, just as really as after human cohabitation. At the same time, once this fatigue has worn off, the fact of having had communion with Deity is quite as much a source of health and cheerful satisfaction as the normal performance of human functions, and conversely, the occurrence of any hindrance to the natural release of energy along lines of religious devotion is liable to be followed by malaise.

Three qualifications to the above statement must, however, be made. First, the total cessation of all sex-experiences is not a necessary condition of any numinous experience. It may be that a specially high degree of it is more easily attainable by those who habitually repress and sublimate sex, but it would certainly not be true that only celibates could have this specially high degree of experience, since happily married persons of both sexes often possess a very intense and sincere spiritual life. Second, repression and attempted sublimation do not necessarily lead to religious experience. They sometimes merely have the effect of forcing sexual thoughts into the foreground of consciousness, with the result that the pious individual is plagued and distressed by lascivious mental images.   Special training and direction are needed if the desired result is to be achieved.   Third, in a certain number of cases sublimation does not seem to lead to a successful result at all, and in these cases there is no numinous experience.   The whole of the libido is expended upon marital or family duties or upon manual or mental labour, and the individual has little or no direct sense of the presence or being of God along intuitional lines, even though he or she may be in no way antagonistic to religion, and may even accept rational accounts of it, and perform religious acts in conformity to authority.

2. *Lapses and Vicissitudes*

When we give our attention to the records of numinous experience we cannot fail to observe that there are a number of curious lapses in the working of the religious consciousness.   It is found to be subject to (1) Periodicity, (2) interruption, (3) atrophy, (4) destruction, and (5) development.   It appears to be absent in certain cases, and in others to be disguised under a different name, so that in these latter cases the absence is only apparent, not real.   We possess analogies to these phenomena in connection with other human faculties such as the perception of colour and sound, and physical health is more intimately connected with our sense perceptions than we like to think.

We will begin with a consideration of the phenomena connected with *Periodicity*.   It has often been pointed

out that the whole life of nature is dominated by the
existence of periodic events. Within the atom there
seem to be rhythms in the movement of the minute
bodies of which it is composed. The path of the
earth round the sun leads to the yearly recurrence of
the seasons. The rotation of the earth produces
successive days. The phases of the moon are recurrent,
and though artificial light has made these phases
to-day less noticeable, human life is still largely
influenced by lunar movements. The presupposition
of periodicity is indeed fundamental to our very conception of life, and but for periodicity the very means
of measuring time as a quantity would be absent.
Even our own bodily life, with its recurrent heart-
beats and breathings is essentially periodic. The
sexual emotions are subject to rhythms, varying
according to age and sex. The movement of a muscle
is accompanied by an electrical discharge followed by
a reaction, and repeated use of the same muscle leads
ultimately to a state of fatigue in which the muscle
refuses to act until it has rested. Similarly the performance of a mental function such as attention or
concentration results in fatigue to the brain mechanism,
involving what we call the wandering of attention.
The power to attend varies according to the age,
health, and training of the individual concerned. In
the puppy, the child, the sick and weary, and the
uneducated the power of concentration is weak,
though we generally accept the fact that it is capable
of being trained and strengthened; but of its inter-
mittent nature there can be no question, and it is
equally certain that with education it tends to become

less fortuitous and variable, and more strictly periodic, while the periods of concentration increase in length.

Periodicity is fundamental to certain departments of mathematics, and in art pattern depends on it. It is less evident but no less certain that periodicity is a factor involved in the making of ritual, and so of religious observance. Not only do the movements of the heavenly bodies control the recurrence of the seasons and tides, with the corresponding tendency to the formation of a calendar of nature-festivals, but the recurrence of the days of memorial for departed persons, the anniversaries of their deaths, produces periodicity in the cultus of departed spirits. And further; it has been pointed out that the expectation of these recurrent anniversaries produces a very interesting condition which is called a "presentation." The approach of the day of ceremony, and the delay in its arrival, cause an intensification of desire. The active satisfaction of the desire is blocked. The thing delayed, expected, and waited for becomes increasingly a source of value, and precipitates into what is called an "idea," the projected shadow of an unaccomplished action.[1]

The more intense one's religious experience the more is its rhythmic nature likely to be felt. Anyone who has taken the trouble to note down the frequency or infrequency with which any given individual readily performs certain acts of devotion will have found that it is possible in some cases to construct a curve showing either very regular alternation, or else one in which the alternations become less and less frequent and the

[1] See Jane Harrison, *Ancient Art and Ritual.*

periods intervening longer and longer. Sometimes the exact opposite is the case. The points begin by being a long distance apart and the frequency increases with varying rapidity up to a certain point, where it either maintains itself or falls back to a middle point at which it finds that it can maintain itself in a condition of stability, or from which it diminishes again until it reaches zero. The truth of this is confirmed by the experience of nearly every man and woman who has tried to practise religious devotion. The swing of the pendulum governs the whole of human life. Hunger and satiety, sleep and waking, exertion and repose, excitement and relaxation, enthusiasm and indifference, follow each other with almost the certainty, if without the exact regularity, of day and night and the revolving seasons. It would be strange, therefore, if so fundamental a human characteristic as religion should fail to be influenced by this deep-seated phenomenon.

The great historical religions have been well aware of the phenomena above described, and have taken account of them in seeking to guide and direct the lives of their adherents. Their leaders have again and again warned the devotee that he must be prepared to experience periods of spiritual dryness and coldness. They have pointed out that the life of the great mystics has shown oscillations between exaltation and depression, and that weaker souls can hardly hope to escape that with which even stronger souls have at times been acutely afflicted.

The value of a proper recognition of the phenomena of periodicity to the minister of religion must be

obvious.   Without it his pastoral theology must be a
mutilated study, and his shepherding of souls fraught
with unexpected pain and disappointment.   But the
evidential importance of the phenomena is still more
important.

It is not necessary that the religious consciousness
should be continuous in order to demonstrate the
reality of the object of which it claims to be aware.
On the contrary, if it be a new or comparatively new
development, it may be something which is having to
struggle in order to find a firm footing.   It seems in
the light of anthropology that it is rather a late development, and the study of childhood on the whole confirms
this.   Now a new element is extremely fragile and
liable to be swamped in competition.   Unless it has
a strong utilitarian value it will suffer acutely, and
will be like a precious flower, growing up amid the
traffic of some public highway, always in peril of
being trodden down and crushed out of existence.

3. Interruption

It may be better to give this title to the periods of
coldness or indifference, when they are of considerable
and uneven length.   We are here dealing with something much more serious than mere oscillation.   It is
beyond dispute that human beings seldom remain
throughout life in steady contact with all points in
their environment.   Attention may shift curiously
with changing circumstances.   The problem is not
by any means one which concerns religion alone.
Large sections of human society live in a state of more
or less permanent dissociation from things of which

there is no reason to doubt the value, truth, or beauty. Absence of an aesthetic sense is very widespread. Many savages, as well as many civilised persons, seem to have no appreciation of natural scenery, and do not care for flowers. The taste for good music, literature and pictures is very unevenly distributed. In spite of the indisputable merits of cleanliness and a devotion to hygiene, the majority of human beings who inhabit the planet are still both coarse and dirty in their habits. Indifference to social and political issues is both fitful and widespread. There have been periods of history during which the general average of attention to some important topic has fallen conspicuously low, while attention to some other no less important topic has at the same time been high. Within the same human life there may be and usually are a number of phases of experience. Thus an individual may in one phase read diligently a particular class of novel or attend concerts frequently, but in another may never buy or borrow a single piece of fiction or go out of the way to hear a note of orchestral music. Such a change does not postulate the unreality of novels, or make the achievements of musicians a mere delusion, but only involves a shifting of the centre of attention and interest. No individual in the course of his life can hope to taste the whole of human experience. He is bound by the limits of age, health, income and capacity, and either voluntarily or by force of circumstances makes a selection. The intense specialisation and the fierce competition of much modern life tend to narrow the average range of experience. It is probable that our more leisurely forefathers had a greater wholeness of outlook and were in touch with life at more points than we moderns, who live at a much higher rate of speed and are much more dependent, through specialisation, upon the activities of others. It is true, of course, that in principle the spirit of religion should permeate all departments of life, just as the appreciation of beauty and the arts should do. But the intensity of modern specialisation, and the pace of much organised urban activity tend to produce a generation of human beings, absorbed, narrow, preoccupied, and inattentive (very often through fatigue or strain) to any interest, however weighty or important, which lies just outside their direct line of action.

Considerable importance is attributed to the cases of certain blind deaf mutes who in the course of their education have been introduced to the ideas of religion and who have responded to them in so remarkable a way that their response has been taken as strong evidence for the correctness of the religious reaction to life. The chief of these cases is that of Helen Keller. She was an American girl who was born as a perfectly normal child, but lost three of her five senses at the age of nineteen months, touch and smell alone remaining. It is naturally very difficult to know how much of her later reactions is to be set down to the revival of memories of the first nineteen months, but it seems quite clear that when at the age of six her education was taken in hand by a Miss Anna Sullivan, she was in the curious position of a small anthropoid animal, fierce, ignorant and in almost every respect totally undeveloped   Her only assets were an intensification of her two remaining senses proportionate to the absence or rather removal of the other three.   The process of educating

Helen proceeded by means of touch, and it seems almost incredible that after long years of patient teaching, this female defective should have been converted into a mature woman of great mental brilliance and varied interests. It is true that Miss Keller was a woman of exceptional mentality, and that in any one less naturally gifted such a process of education would not be likely to have yielded such remarkable results; but we have here to do with a person who is at any rate mentally quite normal, and only deprived of the ordinary means of contact with the external world in the same way in which the celebrated Professor Fawcett was deprived after the accident which destroyed his sight, the only difference being that Helen Keller's deprivation was more complete, and occurred in infancy, so that the ordinary process of education had not only not begun, but was actually handicapped by the restriction of her points of contact with the external world to two-fifths of the normal.

With the general features of her culture we are not here concerned, but only with the fact on which much stress has been laid that she very naturally developed a strong interest in·religion. It must be pointed out, however, that her isolation from the world did not involve a formation of a natural theology within her as she slowly regained contact. It is definitely asserted that when the idea of God was introduced to her it corresponded to nothing in her internal experience. This at least is what we are told by M. Henry, a French psychologist who has studied her case and compared it with those of certain Europeans presently to be described. Miss Keller's own account, however, published in 1927, is that as a little child she was not immediately introduced to Christian theism, but that when she began to question her teacher as to the cause of the existence of the various objects which she could touch and smell, she was told that they were made by Mother Nature, and she adds that at that time she believed that every object she touched was alive and self-conscious. She says that as she grew older she began to reason about the various objects which she touched, and that she noticed a difference between the behaviour of human beings, the behaviour of what we call inanimate objects and the processes of nature. She relates how she was puzzled at the order and sequence of natural objects in the country, at the confusion in the elements which sometimes terrified her and at the wanton destruction of beautiful and ugly, useful and unpleasant, righteous and wicked, without apparently any discrimination. She says that she failed to understand how "a blind mass of irresponsible forces could create and keep alive, destroy and renew and maintain an unfailing succession of rhythms, seasons and generations." She declares that she felt that Nature was no more concerned with her than with a twig or a fly, and that this awoke in her something akin to resentment. It appears from M. Henry's narrative that she put to her instructress the same sort of questions about Deity that any clever child is in the habit of putting: "If God made everything, who made God?" and "If God is good why does he allow hurtful things to happen?" In her own narrative she hints at this and says that when she enquired about God she was baffled, and that the replies of her friends, who were obviously typical Christian theists, seemed inconclusive, but that Phillips Brooks conveyed to her a message in the terms of the fourth Gospel which greatly helped her, though she says that she could not form any clear idea of the relation between this divine love and the material world. She says quite candidly that she was not especially enthusiastic about the Bible stories and thought that the Old Testament Genesis narratives were very similar to Greek and Roman myths, and that the Book of Revelation seemed to her too fierce to be really compatible with the teaching of Christ.

Her real illumination, she says, came to her not so much from book or teaching as from a sudden realisation of what she calls "the realness of my soul and its sheer independence of all conditions of place and body." This came to her after a lesson upon Athens which was followed in her by a sudden vivid piece of visualisation, "a bright amazing realisation which seemed to catch my mind and set it ablaze." She says that the discovery that what she calls her soul could transcend space and time suddenly helped her to a realisation of how Deity could dwell in all the universe simultaneously, and she adds: "If this (my transcendence) were true, how much more could God, the uncircumscribed Spirit, cancel the harms of nature . . . and reach out to his children."

From this time she says that her interest in spiritual subjects grew, but that she was still bewildered and dissatisfied by what she was told about the Bible, obviously in a fundamentalist milieu. At the age of thirteen she met an old German disciple of Swedenborg and from him she learned to appreciate the system of the Scandinavian mystic. In the present century and in England Swedenborg is not often read, but we need to remember that in the earlier years of the nineteenth century he was much respected as a prophet and praised by such widely different types as Emerson, Thomas Carlyle, Henry James, Henry Ward Beecher, Elizabeth Barrett Browning, S. T. Coleridge, and Whittier. It will be seen that four of these were Americans, and this may serve to indicate to some extent the reason for Miss Keller's choice. She was living in a society which admired Swedenborg, and in a generation for which he seemed to have a message. It would be too great a task to evaluate the worth of Swedenborg's alleged revelations, and also irrelevant to the present issue. The main point seems to be that Helen Keller at the period of adolescence was brought into contact with this curious system and came to organise her religious life around it. Her account of herself in later years would seem to show that this rather fanciful interpretation of Christianity was superimposed upon a much simpler appreciation of the teaching and personality of the Jesus of the Synoptic Gospels, and that its attractiveness to her is quite easily accounted for by her blindness, which, as she says, has made everything in the natural world as vague and remote from her senses as spiritual things seem to the minds of most people. To her Swedenborg's assertions do not possess, as they seem to do to most of us, an air of crude certainty, but are a string of mystical symbols whereby he expresses the reality of certain mental qualities and values. She concludes "I cannot imagine myself without religion. I could as easily fancy a living body without a heart." And in the autobiography of her later years, "Midstream," she shows close acquaintance with modern revolutionary movements of thought in Russia, and refers with perfect tranquillity to the work of Lenin, apparently undisturbed by his hatred of that element of mystical religion which is the mainspring of her own life. She can afford to be generous and to see the positive contributions of people differing widely from herself, and thus far her religion is so natural as to be strong evidence for the correctness of the theistic attitude to life. It cannot be said, however, that she evolved this attitude entirely within herself, unaided and untaught. The most that we can say is that Christian theism, plus a certain awakening self-consciousness, seemed to her to provide a correct explanation of life, and that she got from it a sense of satisfaction which is often described as one of the most important elements in the phenomenon of conversion.

Besides the case of Helen Keller, other similar cases are

recorded of perhaps less gifted individuals who have been restored to contact with the outer world by similar processes. Thus, between 1837 and 1838, an institute at Bruges received a child of nine, Anna Tennerman, who was deaf, dumb, and almost blind, but who was taught to read, to write in Flemish, and to knit; and more or less contemporary with the case of Miss Keller is that of Laura Bridgman, a girl of seven years old from the State of New Hampshire, U.S.A., who at the age of $2\frac{1}{2}$ had lost sight, speech, hearing, and smell, but who was restored to contact by the work of a Dr. Howe, and, though less accomplished than Helen Keller, became a sufficiently remarkable woman to astonish those who afterwards visited her, among them Charles Dickens and Longfellow the poet. Another case is that of Marie Heurtin, who was born in 1885 at Vertou in France. This child was blind, deaf, and dumb from birth, and, owing to the poverty of her parents, remained in isolation from the world until she was ten. In her case no memory of sight, speech, or sound was possible. Nevertheless, in the hands of the Sisters of La Sagesse at Larnay, Marie Heurtin learnt to speak and to listen by touch, to express her thoughts in writing, and to acquire a general notion of the world, which, though less rich and varied than that of Miss Bridgman or Miss Keller, was yet extraordinary. M. Henry insists that in these three important cases the idea of Deity did not rise spontaneously in the minds of the patients, but was an artificial grafting, the work of patient educative toil which happened to be destined to a complete success. It is most important, in view of his comment, to judge these cases fairly. Those who are advocates for the truth of religion have pointed to them with pride as showing how naturally persons deprived of the ordinary means of contact with the external world take to the ideas of religion and find rest and satisfaction when these are presented to them, and they are certainly justified in so doing. It must be admitted, however, that not one of these cases can furnish us with any evidence of the spontaneous expression of an intuitive belief. This negative evidence is not, of course, conclusive, because we have no reason to suppose either that such intuitions inevitably arise very early, or that the cases in question would, if they had been normal ones, have manifested intuitive perception to any marked degree; nor do we know what would have been the behaviour of some of the great mystics of the world if they had lost three or more of their senses at an early age, or had been born as blind deaf mutes. We cannot, therefore, lay very much stress on the cases quoted above, except as demonstrating that in the case of three female children of different classes, nationalities, and natural endowments, taken, it seems, almost at random, there is evidence that the simple elements of Christian theism provided them with satisfaction and furnished them with an adequate centre round which to organise life. We cannot say what would have happened in the case of male children, nor can we say that at the present time the number of cases available for investigation is sufficiently large to justify us in drawing any very decisive conclusions. We can only wait and observe, assuming that, in the course of centuries, other cases of a similar sort will arrive. The most we can say is that in the only three cases so far capable of scientific observation those who were responsible for the teaching did not find it impossible to lay a foundation of theistic belief, and that in one of the three there has been a very rich growth of religious activity.

4. Development and Atrophy

The existence of things which are real is obviously in no way dependent upon their apprehension by living beings. We will illustrate this by a few examples.

If we were to collect a roomful of colour-blind people, and then introduce a scarlet geranium in full bloom, it would make no difference to the fact of the colour of the flower that no one in the room could see it. If we were to write out a succession of notes of music ending with high B♭ at concert pitch, it would make no difference to the reality of the possible existence of such a sound as high B♭ that very few persons could ever have heard it sung by a human voice. Similarly the reality of the note actually emitted by a bat in flight is not affected by the fact that it is inaudible to many persons, few human ear-drums being constructed or capable of being trained to register its vibrations. Again, very many fine pieces of craftsmanship are quite beyond the performance of ordinary human beings, but only become possible as the result of prolonged training, and even then demand a certain initial amount of natural ability. The mathematical faculty appears to be developed from primitive instinct, which is able in certain cases only to count up to four. It makes no difference to the truth of a mathematical formula or equation in algebra that a savage is incapable of understanding it. Moreover, the apprehension of a real fact may disappear from the consciousness, without affecting its reality. It makes no difference to the fact of the parentage of a calf that if during the first few days of its life it is prevented from sucking from its mother it does not afterwards begin to do so, nor is the maternal relationship of certain chickens affected by the fact that if they have been shut away from the mother hen who hatched them for eight or ten days after they have broken out of the shell, they will run away from her instead of obeying her call. There are many facts which are indisputably true, but of which the greater part of the human race is ignorant, unaware, or apt to be forgetful.

It is necessary therefore to distinguish clearly between (1) a fact which is real, (2) a fact which is recognised naturally by all, (3) a fact which is recognised naturally by the majority, (4) a fact which is recognised naturally only by a few and by the rest of mankind only as the result of training, (5) an error or misbelief or misreading of fact formerly an object of universal belief, but slowly ceasing to be such as knowledge advances.

Now it will be plain that there will be periods in human history when fact and non-fact will alike be the objects of human belief, owing to the artificial training of human minds which produces or strengthens beliefs. An actual belief on the part of a person who is, according to medical tests, apparently sane may thus be due to the training of his mind and nervous system, which will continue to function even in the absence of a fact to correspond to the belief; and a person who in childhood has been trained in an erroneous belief will continue (sometimes fiercely) to defend that belief even after its falsity has been demonstrated to him, because the demonstration of falsity conflicts with his previously formed mental habits. On the other hand the perception of a fact, the probability of which is capable of being demonstrated, especially on the grounds of coherence and congruity, may easily be absent from the mind of a person who has been trained to ignore it, or who has been submitted to powerful suggestions that it does not exist. The most striking instance of mental atrophy is that to which Charles Darwin confessed in the now famous extract from one of his letters. "My mind has become a kind of machine for grinding general laws out of large collections of facts, and I lament that I have lost all interest in poetry and music."[1] We may say, then, with justice, that if the probability of a fact be capable of establishment whether on the grounds of congruity or coherence or for some other reason, the absence of the apprehension of that fact from certain persons will not necessarily render that fact unreal, since it may be possible both to develop and to destroy the capacity to apprehend a fact, the reality of which may be shown upon other grounds to be either probable or improbable.

It seems well to make a few observations upon the alleged decline on the part of the human race in its interest in religion. We have of course to take into account the natural rhythms and fluctuations in interest which always mark the life of man. He is sometimes frivolous and sometimes serious, sometimes mainly emotional, at others mainly rationalistic. The present decline may then prove to be merely a case of rhythm. It seems, however, more probable that in the present case it is partly due to a progressive change. A narrower view (possibly also an inferior one) as to what is meant by religion is probably giving way to a

---

[1] Darwin mentions in another letter (Francis Darwin, *Life and Letters of Darwin* (1887), Vol. I, p. 101) that there was a time when the beauty of nature inspired him with a sense of cosmic awe, but that his abstract studies have tended gradually to deprive him of this sense, and its disappearance he regards as a real loss.

wider one, and curiously enough the wider one is not merely in harmony with the definition which we have elsewhere proposed for adoption,[1] but it is also singularly in harmony with that indicated by Christ. It needs to be remembered that the early Christians were commonly called ἄθεοι by their enemies, a somewhat startling fact, but clear evidence that their view of religion was sufficiently different from that of the gentile world around them for it to be hardly recognisable as religion. It is probable that this was partly due to their inheritance from Judaism of a pure spiritual monotheism, but at any rate it remains a fact. The world of conventional religion has reacted largely since then in the gentile direction, so that the swing of the pendulum once again towards the opposite point is not immediately recognisable as due to the actual triumph of Christian principles insensibly propagated by the churches and schools of organised Christianity better than they knew. The use of the term "religious" in a narrower sense has indeed in the intervening centuries become so marked that a modern writer has even ventured to say that the real question for us is not whether a man is religious, but rather, "where does he stand?"[2] Personally I should prefer to say that where a man stood with regard to the totality of things was a very good index as to the nature of his religious faith, but the fussy observance of religious institutions without very much thought and mainly from the desire to acquire some sort of merit, or from the fear of failing to propitiate

[1] In my *Man and Deity* (1933).
[2] Keyserling, *The Recovery of Truth.*

a touchy and possibly malevolent spirit is only to be religious in the narrower sense of δεισιδαιμονεστέρος, and as such deserves reprobation quite as much as it did in the days of Theophrastus. It is in any case a very different thing from the practice of pious habits for the purpose of building character and of maintaining a continuous and habitual relationship with Deity.

5. *Destruction*

The importance of these general considerations becomes clearer when we come to consider a definite situation which has arisen in the modern world. The political exploitation of an organised religious system in the interests of absolute government has led within the last one hundred and fifty years to violent attacks upon religion in general by the opponents of political tyranny. The events of the French Revolution are not very well known to many persons to-day, but those of the Russian Revolution are familiar to most, and the policy of anti-clericals in France is only a continuation in a milder form of that pursued in the days of the Terror. The avowed policy of the French and Russian extremist has been to train up a generation of men and women who have definitely been taught that religion is falsehood and the idea of Deity a delusion.

A child of eleven wrote to the editor of a Bolshevik newspaper printed in a Canadian city to ask how the idea of God arose, and the editor replied: "It was a myth made up some years ago by the bosses to frighten the people into obeying; they were told if they did not God would punish them." The crudity and

inaccuracy of Bolshevik propaganda must not, however, blind us to its widespread influence and plausi-
bility. We are bound to admit that religion has been
exploited in the interests of tyranny, and is probably
being still so exploited. It is, therefore, not surprising
that ignorant persons will rashly assume that religion
is the invention of tyrants, whether priests or bosses.
It is idle to lay the blame entirely on the Catholic
priest, because on the whole his influence has been no
more dangerous than that of the Protestant boss;
and to confuse religion with its exploitation is to do
it a manifest injustice. Nevertheless the success of
propaganda is bound to be encouranged by: (1) the
weakening of the theistic sense in a mechanised urban
culture and (2) the inertia and stagnation of religious
institutions. Persons in whom the theistic sense is
weak and who are unacquainted with any sound
philosophy which can help to strengthen it, naturally
fall an easy prey to any agitator who tells them that
they have been deceived. It is hardly their fault,
for they have very often had little or no satisfactory
teaching, and the only general world-view which has
come to them has perhaps been that of the communist
international.

The experiment of what is called secular state
education, which is in progress in a number of countries,
is producing, then, a type of human being sometimes
trained definitely in an anti-religious attitude. It
does not help our case to deny that the system has
achieved a measure of success. Any system of course
can succeed which adopts an educational policy of
exclusion. It would be interesting, though rather

cruel, to experiment over a wide enough area in the exclusion of music and the pictorial arts from school life. No one on principle would be allowed to draw or paint, to play a musical instrument or to sing. The effect would be no doubt the disappearance of music and other arts from the greater part of the population affected, and their surreptitious practice by a minority; while the cause of art and music might be set back for some generations. But one cannot for ever purge any people of that which is a natural growth, and the attempt to do so only results on the one hand in the crippling and maiming of the human spirit, and on the other hand in smouldering rebellion.[1]

It is vain to fetter human speculation and inquiry, and to bar a rising generation from knowing anything about what its forefathers have thought. It is true, as we have seen, that in the writings of some Greek freethinkers we find religion challenged; but it is significant that by far the larger mass of philosophical writing is on the side of a mystical theism. The truth is that the question is much less whether Deity exists than what we mean when we speak of Deity. Those who have trained themselves in friendly communion with the invisible supra-personal spirit of whom the intuitionists speak will be almost constrained to smile at arguments about Him, or at the spectacle of those who though knowing Him fail to recognise Him or perhaps choose to describe Him by some other name. Probably the best conclusion which can be made to

[1] N.B.—A friend has suggested that Quakers are very unmusical because music has been on principle banished by them from their services. But I cannot vouch for this. Actually the largest Friends' Meeting House in the United States is furnished with an extremely fine organ.

this section is a quotation of the considered opinion of a Quaker astronomer of this century.[1]

"The heart of the question is commonly put in the form 'Does God really exist?' It is difficult to set aside this question without being suspected of quibbling: but I venture to put it aside because it raises so many unprofitable side issues, and at the end it scarcely reaches deep enough into religious experience. Among leading scientists to-day I think about half assert that the aether exists and the other half deny its existence; but as a matter of fact both parties mean exactly the same thing, and are divided only by words. Ninety-nine people out of a hundred have not seriously considered what they mean by the term 'exist', not how a thing qualifies itself to be labelled real. Theological or anti-theological argument to prove or disprove the existence of a deity seems to me to occupy itself largely with skating among the difficulties caused by our making a fetish of this word. It is all so irrelevant to the assurance for which we hunger. In the case of our human friends we take their existence for granted, not caring whether it is proven or not. Our relationship is such that we could read philsophical arguments designed to prove the non-existence of each other, and perhaps even be convinced by them—and then laugh together over so odd a conclusion. I think that it is something of the same kind of security we should seek in our relationship with God. The most flawless proof of the existence of God is no substitute for it; and if we have that relationship the most convincing disproof is turned harmlessly aside. If I may say it with reverence, the soul and God laugh together over so odd a conclusion."

It seems appropriate to refer here to the classification of knowledge put forward by Spinoza, not in order to

[1] Sir Arthur Eddington, *Swarthmore Lecture*, pp. 42-43.

endorse every detail, but for the purpose of pointing out that so acute and independent a thinker did not disparage but rather emphasised strongly the validity of immediate experience. Spinoza was neither a Christian nor an orthodox Jew, and therefore in quoting him we cannot be accused of employing the services of one who is prejudiced in our favour. He claims to distinguish three kinds of knowledge: the first of which he calls ordinary sense-perception (*cognitio primi generis*); the second, rational knowledge (*ratio*) that derived from inference; and the third, intuitive knowledge, (*scientia intuitiva*), or an immediate internal conviction of the nature of telepathy. It is evident from his description of the latter that he regarded it as on a different plane from the first, and that he, in common with a number of other great minds, laid claim to the enjoyment of a number of lofty and intimate experiences, which in their fulness could not be enjoyed by the multitude, nor even by many clever and intelligent persons. It is perfectly true that persons who are endowed with large or frequent gifts of religious insight are as rare as geniuses of any other sort, and that the prophet, poet, and mystic are not fruits which hang on every human family tree. Yet mild mystical experiences, chance flashes of prophetic fire, and brief moments of poetic inspiration come to nearly everyone, even to those mute and inglorious persons who can never tell what they have seen; and such relatively faint and fleeting intuitions are to most of us the commonest evidence which we feel inclined to adduce for the existence of Deity.

VALIDITY OF IMMEDIATE EXPERIENCE

The one all-important question to be decided is the *validity* of this *intuitive* knowledge. It has been challenged of late by a school of continental psychologists whose leader has put forward what is known as the projection theory. According to this, mental images are frequently the results of our desires; the wish is father to the thought. A child desires something intensely; it therefore weaves a make-believe situation in which it possesses the object of its desires. Another is afraid; it therefore invents some phantasy to alleviate its fears. Childless women weave pictures of dream-children. So it is argued, mankind in the midst of an unfriendly universe has believed and still believes to a great extent like a frightened child. It has projected its desire for protection into the external world, and has woven the phantasy of a Heavenly Father. The ruthless cruelty of this theory must not prejudice us against its brilliancy. That we do sometimes weave phantasies it is idle to deny; and that they sometimes have a powerful influence upon our conduct also cannot be denied. This, however, need not involve us in the conclusion that all the mental pictures which we form are pathetic illusions, mere pieces of self-deception.

Let us admit that the objectification of Deity by the mind of man is *in form* of the nature of a projection. That in itself does not invalidate it. Every objectification which we make to ourselves is a projection from inside ourselves. Our egos, A, B, C, D, etc., say that an object X exists outside them, and proceed to describe it in symbols derived from the previous experience of A, B, C, D, etc. But this process does not in itself *prove* the existence of X, whether a table or a god. Either may be a mere projection and no more. The test is whether the projection (as has been well said) hits something,[1] or rather whether the thing which we perceive as a projection can hit us.

Thus to reduce any single item in our experience, *i.e.* Deity, to a mere projection is to strike a blow at the validity of all knowledge of things external to our egos.

Plainly, however, it must be our business to distinguish, and to find some canons by which we may be able to distinguish, between those of our mental pictures which are phantasies and those which correspond to something real. The necessity for such canons is one which concerns not only religion but all human interests. If we have no means of testing the validity of our various sense-impressions, how can we tell that we are not being deceived at every moment of our lives and that science and the daily newspaper are providing us with anything more than pleasant (or unpleasant) dreams? It is usual to say that the all-important test is that of *coherence*. Obviously there are some impressions which we receive the moment we open our eyes after birth which are prior to any reasoning, and which we are bound to accept without exactly knowing why. We may reason about these afterwards, but we cannot get behind them, for they are what are called ultimates. Now we are aware that there are a number of persons in the world whose

[1] So W. R. Matthews, *Religion and the Modern Mind.*

primary sensations which are the data for their subsequent reasoning are not those of ordinary normal
individuals. Either we feel that they may be super-
normal, and that their experiences may in this case
be genuine and none the worse for their abnormality,
though not easily or quickly to be authenticated by
ordinary folk; or else something is wrong with their
wits, causing a disturbance, which is then to be
regarded as being due to the influence of a drug like
mescalin, to toxic poisoning as in the case of some
person in delirium, to ante- or post-natal malformation
of the brain, or to some organic disease, as *e.g.* in the
case of a person suffering from tertiary syphilis.
Seeing double or seeing or hearing things which are
not there is thus a pathological condition which the
ordinary person claims to be able to detect because
the subject of it is obviously out of touch with reality.
His visions and voices do not fit in with the rest of his
surroundings as observed by ordinary people. Sometimes he is the victim of a hysterical attack; yet the
strange thing is that prophecy and intuitive visionary
perception closely resemble hysteria. G. B. Shaw is
correct in his famous delineation of Mrs. George when
he makes her declare that something gets into her and
says itself. Such persons are ostensibly as prone to
talk sense as to babble nonsense. Now it must be
granted we think that a very large number of persons
possess in some form or other, or claim to possess,
the consciousness of Deity, and are therefore claiming
to experience sensations which are not universal, but
equally it must be granted that many such persons
(though admittedly not all of them) appear in other

respects to be neither insane nor hysterical nor under the influence of a toxic poison or a drug. The presumption is therefore not unreasonable that since they are perceiving things correctly in ninety-nine instances, they are perceiving correctly in the hundredth instance. It is true that persons are to be found who are described as perfectly sane in all matters except one, but it is discovered on examination that, however normal they may be in ninety-nine cases, the hundredth case, in which they prove pathological, distorts the other ninety-nine parts of their experience. Now it can hardly be denied that the assertion say of fifty Christians that they are personally in touch with the Being described in the opening words of the Lord's Prayer is compatible with their being sane in all other respects. If, however, in this one particular we were to regard them as pathological we should then expect to find that the effect of their belief was in some way to distort or vitiate the rest of their conduct. But this cannot be said to be the case, since the examination of fifty such persons will in all probability be found to lead to the conclusion that, whereas in a few cases the belief will be a mere verbal expression of formal assent, in the remainder it will be found to have a positive and definitely steadying and enriching effect upon conduct. It cannot, therefore, be said that this particular religious belief when actively professed has a distorting effect upon the minds of ordinary citizens. It is not my purpose at this point to endeavour to show that either all or even the majority of the beliefs of Christians as traditionally expressed are necessarily capable of passing the test

of rational coherence. Some of them are, some of
them are probably not. All that matters at this
point is to demonstrate that one single important
example of the holding of a belief that the individual
is in touch with a real divine Person is compatible
with sane and coherent behaviour.

There are, however, other reasons for rejecting the
theory of mere compensatory projection as being
capable of accounting for all our unusual intuitions.

In the first place it has been recently pointed out[1]
with great clarity that the following four propositions
are indisputable, *i.e.*:—

(1) That if religion be ascribed to any universal
     aspect of mind and then treated as illusion, all
     knowledge is then exposed to the same charge—
     which is absurd.

(2) That if our absolute values and ideal standards
     are the mere singularities of a particular biped
     and not manifestations of the ultimate reality,
     again all knowledge is impossible—which is
     equally absurd.

(3) That if religion be illusion, then no satisfactory
     explanation can be given as to why it has wrought
     so long and so effectively, nor why, if it be thought
     to have arisen from mass-feeling, it is held to
     have developed into the one thing which is
     regarded as effectively opposed to the mass
     mind, since "nothing is more certain than that
     the Sacred claims to have its sanctions in itself,
     and that it is corrupted when its sanction is
     submission to the opinions of the herd."

[1] Oman, *The Natural and the Supernatural.*

(4) That if the mechanical mode of behaviour has always been known by man, and if reality corresponds to it alone, then there is no satisfactory answer to the three questions:—

(a) How did man come to apply so extensively the wrong method to the world when he knew the right one?

(b) Why is it that imagination as a practical faculty is only of value so long as it deals with realities and is not mere fantasy-weaving?

(c) And again, since man is a part and product of the world, what were its mechanical ways doing when they created him to contradict them, if nothing but the mechanical exists?

In the second place, if the object of religious phantasy, so called, be the projection of a protective Deity, this does not explain how it comes to pass that the picture of Deity is in the majority of cases not at all like the picture which a frightened child or even a human being seeking a protective parent would invent for itself. Thus when an unknown religious poet puts into the mouth of his hero the words: "Though he slay me yet will I trust him," it seems difficult to believe that he was making a picture of his own desires by saying in the face of an unfriendly universe "yet will I trust him." Again, by no means the majority of the deities pictured by religious persons are tender; indeed their attempts seem to indicate that man, so far from reading his own desires into nature, has taken nature at her face value with her apparent ruthlessness and carelessness of individual life, and accepted it as a fact. Indeed, if the "Benevolent Parent" projection were the natural explanation of the idea of Deity, we should expect to find it more widely distributed, and much more universal than it is; whereas it is so limited, and its maintenance requires for its justification so much patient and persistent faith that it is not surprising that many have declared that we should not know of the Fatherhood of Deity except by a divine revelation, or at any rate as the result of the work of some prophetic individual possessing exceptional insight, and tested by others through long-term experiment in respect of its validity.

Religious belief, in the sense of belief in Necessary or Self-Existent Being, is logically an inevitable concomitant of reason. In such a sense there can be no atheists or unbelievers. But it needs more than credulity, more than fantasy-weaving, to credit Necessary Being with Christian attributes. It needs faith in the reality of just that element of wise and pain-sharing parenthood which the data of life seem to require, in order that we may make sense of them, yet the reality of which cannot be completely established without trust leading into experience.

The coherence of the system based upon the Gospel of Jesus is great and real, but it is not immediately evident, and needs testing over a considerable area of experience. When so tested it stands where all others fail.

That the sex instinct is closely associated with certain manifestations of the religious consciousness we have already not hesitated to admit. But we must not forget that it is equally associated with the origin

of many other forms of human activity, such as games,
art, poetry, and music. To trace a noble activity
back to a humble origin does not really reveal to us
any deep secret about it. It only tells us about its
humble origin. It is to the highest forms of the
activity itself that we must look for the full explanation
of its meaning.

Broadly speaking, we may say that until recently
there have been three views with regard to intuitive
experience. The *first* of these, which we may call the
traditional one, is that there is a natural world enclosed
within a supernatural order which for short may be
called Deity. These two realms are separate, and the
contact of the one the one with the other through the
mind of the intuitionist is wholly dependent upon the
condescension of Deity: there is, as it were, a miracu-
lous downrush of Deity into the soul which is of the
nature of revelation. The *second* view is that of pure
naturalism. According to this there is no supernatural realm, or if there is (which is a matter of
opinion) we cannot possibly say as a matter of observed
fact that it intervenes in any way in the closer system
of nature. Religious experience must therefore be
capable of explanation as due to the operation of
forces contained within the closed system. The
third view may be called the mediating one. It
avoids dualism, by saying that all is natural and all
supernatural, and that the one is only an intensification
of the other. Religious experience is thus not miracu-
lous in the sense of being an intervention from a totally
distinct order. It is simply a penetration of the finite
and partially spontaneous by That Which brought it

into being and from Which it derives not only its origin but also whatever degree of spontaneity it possesses, and it is thus the reinforcement and heightening of a life already there by a fresh current of life from the original Source; this influx of life being rendered possible by a certain purity and receptive disposition on the part of the spontaneous agent.

It must be admitted that until recently naturalism seemed in a very strong position, firmly entrenched in a world from which the fortuitous element was steadily being banished. Recently, however, there has been a marked tendency to admit that observation has detected and recorded a certain free, fortuitous, and spontaneous element in the minutest forms of matter, and also that the picture of the universe as a closed and monotonously mechanical system is only of the nature of a map, and is arrived at by omitting those features which do not harmonise with such a conception. Hence the tendency towards the qualification of a wholly immanental view of the relation of God to the world, which has been noted elsewhere.

The position then would seem to be that the operation of the brain of the person claiming direct experience may be capable of description by the scientific psychologist in mechanistic terms; yet this description will be only one limited aspect of the experience in question. The other description, that the claimant is in touch with a Wider Self may well be equally true. The case has been well compared by an American psychologist to an account which might be given by a man who had seen the sun for the first time after having lived under abnormal conditions, and given to a company of blind men who had never seen it. The seer would describe quite frankly the bright round object of his vision: but the blind psychologist would say that he could account for the phenomenon by certain conditions prevailing within the eye, "Raised eye-lids, stimulated retina, afferent impulse in the optic nerves, and stimulation of the visual centres in the occipital lobes." Both would be right. The explanation of the psychologist would be correct within its own limits and it could not prove the objective existence of the sun merely by the movements going on within the eye, for it might easily say that these movements produced the appearance of a luminous ball which was therefore a projection from inside the eye. And yet it would be generally admitted that the seer in question really did see the sun.[1]

Another point to be mentioned in this connection is the evidence from the case of a man who has had his leg amputated. It is well known that such a person will under certain conditions experience the hallucination of "feeling his leg," which of course is not there. The hallucination in this instance does not prove that the man is mistaken in supposing that he ever had a leg, but that he formerly had one, and that, however completely the stump may have healed up, it will be impossible in view of the evidence to say that he was born minus a limb. It may well be asserted that the malaise experienced by such large numbers of secularists is not due to the non-existence of Deity, but to the fact that in a society which has amputated its religion there will always be twinges which remind

[1] J. B. Pratt, *The Religious Consciousness*, final chapter.

the sufferers of the existence of something which has been forcibly removed.

There are three other considerations which may be urged in favour of the validity of direct religious experience. *First* we must give full weight to the general value of intuitions in all constructive thought and research. It has been pointed out that in the development of scientific doctrine from scientific data we have actually in principle an appeal to intuition. It would be strange if in our attempts to construct a picture, however provisional, of the whole of reality, we were to find ourselves deprived of this aid.[1] In the *second* place we are faced by the fact that whereas a rationalisation from an isolated experience may well appear somewhat flimsy evidence for the existence of an entity of which many people confess that they are not immediately aware, the spectacle of a multiplicity of experiences leading to similar if not identical forms of rationalisation is too serious evidence to be lightly ignored.[2] In the *third* place it is a singular fact that the direction of the libido upon a religious object is a permanent source of health. It is all very well for a certain type of psychologist to say that this is only another case of the creation of a phantasy love-object in place of a real one. The direction of the libido of a neurotic upon a phantasy, though no rare phenomenon, affords no permanent or assured relief to the sufferer. The dream is liable to be dissolved at any time, and no really solid or satisfactory work can be done by a person who is in a perpetual state of

[1] This argument is less valuable if intuitions be in such cases only apparent and not real.

[2] Thus Thouless, in the concluding chapter of his *Introduction to the Psychology of Religion*.

make-believe. It is otherwise with the healthy and
fit religious person, or with the neurotic who "gets
religion." These find in the maintenance of their
beliefs the very mainstay of their strength and *bien-
être*. A practising psycho-analyst, who maintained
a completely open mind as to the truth or falsehood
of religion, once told Dr. Thouless that in nearly all his
cases he found some religious belief which he did not
touch, because experience had taught him that it was
the strongest force making for the patients' recovery.

There remains, however, the alleged ill-health of the
mystics. This has been so often observed, that
not a few psychologists write off the whole of the
phenomena of intense religious experience as that of
scrupuleux who tend towards hysteria, and who now
and then approximate without ever quite reaching it.
In this matter the alienist seems to find it exceedingly
difficult to keep his balance. He needs to take into
account the association of somewhat similar ill-health
with many types of genius. We do not for that
reason write off all the achievements of genius as
purely pathological states. It is even arguable that
the ill-health of genius is not infrequently the price
paid for concentration leading to achievement; while
it has certainly been pointed out that the ecstasy to
those who experience it is a source, not of weakness
and mental disorder, but (after the exhaustion produced
by the experience has worn off) of unification and
actual increase of mental and bodily strength. For
unusual people intense mystical experience may be a
necessary condition for their best work, and we have
no right to say that it is therefore pathological.
Moreover, though few of us would care to put up with

the discomfort of being a genius, most of us would like to have a streak of genius in our composition. This is no more than to say that few of us would care to endure the strain that some mystics seem to have to experience, and yet the mild amount of alleged direct apprehension of Deity which is our portion is something with which we would not willingly part. It can hardly fail to be recognised that the finest work has been done again and again by the practical mystics, whose beneficent activity has resulted from an invisible urge of a disinterested kind and not from the desire for riches or worldly success.

Yet when all is said, we have to come back to the great mass of normal persons who have never thought of filling up a questionnaire or of writing self-revelations. The evidence of the fit individual who rejoices in serving God and finds his experience strongest when he is in perfect health, and his religious desires at maximum when his powers of mind and body are at their zenith—this evidence is seldom recorded. Even James gives less room to the confessions of the healthy-minded than to those of the twice-born. Yet in the former we are dealing with normal psychology, in the latter with pathology.

To sum up: religious experience may well seem to be discovery or awareness of one's own mental states, the consciousness of powers welling up from within one's self. Yet unless we adopt the (to me at least) impossible attitude that the life of Deity is discontinuous from ours, it seems reasonable to treat the religious interpretation of such experience as the manifestation and activity of that Living Power from which we as human organisms are derived.

THEORY OF IMMEDIATE EXPERIENCES

But it may be said: "Can you talk as glibly as you do about these beliefs as based on experience, when you know very well that the experiences themselves are in some cases described in terms which flatly contradict one another, and which in certain cases cannot possibly be accepted as true descriptions of fact? How can they all be valid? What are we to make of someone who has a vision which says, *Je suis l'Immaculée conception*, and of another, a Protestant, who declares either that Christ has revealed to him the falsity of this particular Roman doctrine, or that the world is to come to an end in a particular year?"

Again it has been pointed out that even so typical a female mystic as Saint Teresa carefully sifted all her experiences, and would not accept any one of them, but rejected it as either a piece of illusion or a work of the devil, or both, unless she found that it left:—

"Peace, calm and good fruits in the soul, and particularly the following three graces of a very high order:—the first a perception of the greatness of God, which becomes clearer to us as we witness more of it: secondly, self-knowledge and humility, as we see how creatures so base as ourselves in comparison with the Creator of such wonders, have dared to offend Him in the past or venture to gaze on Him now: and thirdly, a contempt of all earthly things unless they are consecrated to the service of so great a God."

Plainly the mere sense of the givenness of any alleged private revelation is not a certificate of its truth. It is as well to remember of course that there is not quite as much contradiction between the larger findings of the intuitionists of the various religions as might be expected. In spite of the fact that they bring to their experiences their own dogmatic systems, and in consequence express their self-revelations in terms belonging respectively to such systems, there is, as has already been observed, a considerable elementary agreement between them. At the same time a claim to experience must be subjected to rigid tests before it can be accepted as genuine, and not as self-deception or hallucination. It is worth noting that no organised religious community has been more scrupulous in theory in insisting upon this than the church of Rome; and leaders of her official handbooks of mystical theology will be aware that any claim to private revelations has to submit to severe scrutiny.

It seems desirable to examine closely this Roman Catholic theory of private revelations, partly because the fact that this particular community imposes such a rigid series of tests is in itself remarkable (much more so than if the tests themselves had been propounded by psychologists of Downing Street, Cambridge), partly because some of these tests at any rate seem to furnish general assistance upon the question as to how far the intuitional element in religious knowledge is to be trusted. We will for the moment set on one side the question as to whether there can be such a thing as an authentic revelation at all, and consider merely what is alleged to have taken place; for the classification of this will hold good whether we grant the possibility of revelation or no. Fr. Poulain[1]

---

[1] In his *Grâces d'Oraison*, from which I draw here very largely.

defines a revelation as a mystic state in which Deity is felt to be active upon the soul. It must be observed that in the Bible authentic Hebrew history opens with one private revelation—that made to Abraham; while the New Testament ends with another, or rather with a series. All revelation seems to begin by being private, in the sense that it is not at first officially endorsed by Church or State. At the same time it divides into revelation made to a group and revelation made to an individual. As an example of the former we may take that alleged to have been given to the Christian community at the first Pentecost; of the former, the alleged injunction given to Peter regarding kôsher food, or Mohammed's alleged commission to take an extra wife, or Dr. Marie Stopes' supposed orders to speak to the bishops about birth control.

The official Roman Catholic teaching is that public and universal revelation ended with the apostles, *i.e.* with the giving of what is called the deposit of faith. Since then there has only been private revelation, concerning which certain tests exist for application. There are obvious objections to this hard and fast division, since it assumes the complete authentication of all that has gone before, and thus slurs over the fact that the revelations made to the prophets and to the historical Jesus Himself in the last resort also require authentication, if we are to avoid arguing in a circle, by saying that Christ authenticates the Church and then that the Church authenticates Christ. Plainly the test of free enquiry which Poulain describes as permitted in the case of post-apostolic saints, must also be applied to the Founder of Christianity Himself, if we are to accept Him intelligently for what He claims to be. The division may be arbitrary, but this does not vitiate the tests. Indeed the earlier we carry back our enquiry the more evident it is that scrutiny has always been ruthless and even sometimes unfriendly. We are all familiar with the challenges levelled against many of the Hebrew prophets, from the days of Micaiah ben Imlah and Zedekiah ben Chenaanah to those in which unfriendly critics said that Jesus the prophet of Nazareth had a devil, or was mad, or was beside himself. We remember the injunction in the first of the Johannine epistles to try the spirits, and the shrewd comment in the Didache that he who orders a table in the spirit or stays more than three days when offered hospitality is likely to be a false prophet. Perhaps in later days it was not mere latitudinarian prejudice which led Bishop Butler to say to the founder of methodism:—

"Mr. Wesley, I will deal plainly with you: I once thought you and Mr. Whitfield well-meaning men, but I cannot think so now, for I have heard more of you—matters of fact, sir. And Mr. W. says in his journal: 'There are promises still to be fulfilled in me.'' Sir, the pretending to *extraordinary revelation* and gifts of the Holy Ghost is a horrid thing, a very horrid thing."

The bishop doubtless had in mind the hysterical scenes associated with some of the revival meetings.

We must begin by pointing out that there is a clear distinction between two distinct sorts of revelation, that which must be spoken of, and that which ought not to be spoken of. In other words there is, let us say, the prophetic intuitionist and the reticent intuitionist.[1] Plainly there is a sort of alleged revelation which, though it may have been made to an individual, is clearly felt by the recipient to be meant to be passed on to a group; and there is also that which is given to the individual, which, if he is sincere and modest, he will keep to himself and not boast about. Even in the former case the true prophet feels himself to be a man of unclean lips and stammering tongue, the unworthy instrument whereby the word of the Lord is proclaimed. Once let him become self-confident and proud of his eloquence, and he will probably cease to proclaim the Word of the Lord, and proclaim his own word instead. I think we may say that the second class of revelation corresponds to the "showings" made to Lady Julian of Norwich and other mystics, to the "openings" so frequently referred to by George Fox, and to the "guidance" so often referred to by pious Evangelical Christians.

I will now give the official Roman Catholic tests, without for the moment expressing either agreement or dissent. Belief in special revelations, says Poulain, is not required by the Church even when she approves of them. Such approval can only be regarded as declaring (a) that there is nothing in them contrary to faith and morals, (b) that they may be treated as probable, and may be accepted as such without danger and even with advantage. In order to secure approval it is necessary for it to be established that there is no element of illusion in the experiences in question. Poulain gives thirty-two cases of saints

[1] Do these types possibly correspond to the extravert and introvert of the psychologists?

and pious persons whose private judgment has been privileged in this way. Practically, he adds, in the case of those who have not attained to high sanctity *we can admit that at least three quarters of their revelations are illusions.* He is led to believe that illusion is easier in the case of interior locutions (intellectual or imaginative) than with imaginative visions, since these are much more nearly akin to the ordinary operations of the human mind in which ideas and phrases arise perpetually. If these are clear and sudden, an inexperienced person will conclude that he cannot have produced them himself.

There are it would seem five causes of error which may have had an adverse influence upon the expression of true revelation. These are:—

(*a*) Faulty interpretations which ignore the conditions under which revelation is given.

(*b*) Ignorance of the fact that insight into historic events is often expressed with approximate truth only.

(*c*) The mingling of human activity with supernatural action during the revelation.

(*d*) Subsequent but involuntary modifications made by the person who receives the revelation.

(*e*) Embellishments by secretaries or compilers.

The revelation may be obscure, since God gives at times only a partial comprehension of its import. Moreover, all forecasts of punishments or rewards are conditional, even if they do not appear to be so. Then again, God does not deceive us in modifying certain details in mental visions which He grants to us of historical events. He is like a painter, who in order to excite our piety is content to paint scenes in his own

manner, but without departing too far from the truth.
He is not seeking to satisfy an idle desire for erudition
in history or archaeology, but has a nobler aim,
that of the soul's sanctification. Modifications to an
historical scene are sometimes caused, therefore, with
the object of bringing out the secret meaning of the
event. Symbols too are often used: saints and angels
shew themselves to us with bodies which they do not
in reality possess. Many apparent contradictions
between visions experienced by the saints and prophets
are due to the above, and some are even the fruit of
the pious meditations and contemplations due to the
private individual action of these individuals themselves. We certainly make a mistake in attributing
purely to God the information obtained in a vision,
since during dreams the human mind retains its power
of mingling its own action with the divine. At
times it is the memory which supplies its reflection:
at others, the inventive faculty is at work.

It may be asked: what kind of personal ideas are
we specially inclined to attribute wrongly to divine
influence, either during ecstasy or when in close
communion with God? The answer is:—

(1) ideas which appeal to our own desires.

(2) ideas which are preconceived.

The alleged revelations of Saint Hildegard contain
not only scientific errors but also (doubtless unknown
to her) much which proceeded from her frequent
conversations with the theologians and learned men
of her day, from books that she had read, or the
sermons she had heard.

Subsequent alteration is obviously inevitable when a private revelation is received instantaneously, in which what is called an intellectual locution has to be translated into language in order to be communicated, and in such translations something is often lost or added or transformed. In addition to this, secretaries, chroniclers, or compilers have often been guilty of paraphrasing or altering the communication thus made, either in the interests of embellishment or translation.

Poulain next gives five causes of entirely false revelations.

(a) Deliberate simulation.
(b) An over-lively imagination.
(c) An illusion of the memory, which consists in believing that we recall certain events which never happened.
(d) Diabolical action.
(e) Deliberate falsification by compilers of what was once truly recorded.

The possible causes of illusion and the intrusion of human elements having thus been dealt with, it remains to consider the positive tests by which we may judge whether a private revelation is of divine origin. It might seem in the light of the foregoing considerations that certitude was impossible. This, however, is not the case. In the natural order our senses are subject to many illusions; yet in a multitude of cases we have no doubt that we are not mistaken. In the same way, declares Poulain, we can have complete certainty that intuitions regarding our knowledge of spiritual facts are trustworthy, and he then goes on to enumerate certain tests of certitude. He opens by asking: "What are the credentials of the great Hebrew prophets, and how may we know that they were not deceived or deceivers? What were the indubitable signs of their mission?" The answer begins in a way which does not commend itself, *i.e.* by the certificate of miracles performed by the prophets. We must not, however, on this account dismiss Poulain's tests as unworthy of further attention. He admits that alleged miracles provide a rather abnormal means of deciding the case, and says that the more usual method is the one which discusses the reasons for and against the probability of the truth of the revelation alleged, and this, he says, usually results only in giving us a greater or lesser degree of probability. Whether this is so, he adds, we must not be afraid to own it. The far-reaching importance of this latter admission can hardly be exaggerated. Since, as we have seen, it is not possible to restrict the application of this method, as Rome apparently does, we have here an admission that in the last resort the most vital truths of the Christian faith are made to depend *upon a greater or lesser degree of probability.*

(A) The right course to adopt in judging the evidence is first to obtain detailed information regarding the recipient of the experience, under seven heads of enquiry.

(1) What are the natural qualities and defects, physical, intellectual, and moral, of the person concerned?

(2) What is his degree of education?

(3) Does the account show a talent for composition superior to that attainable by the aid of such natural gift?

(4) What virtues does this person possess, and what was his moral standard both before and after the experience?

(5) Has the experience caused moral and spiritual progress and created a centre of moral energy? Has it inclined the soul towards the solid virtues in a real and durable manner?

(6) Has the experience specially produced humility? (it is a sign of pride and therefore of illusion to have a craving to divulge the graces that we believe ourselves to have received. Humility leads to their concealment, except in cases of real utility, such as those in which a prophet believes himself to be entrusted with a message; even then he must, if he is to be believed, show in all sincerity that he regards himself merely as the mouth of the Lord, and show no sign of self-aggrandisement.)

(7) What extraordinary graces of union with God, or what private revelations has the person believed himself to have previously received, and what has been the verdict concerning them?

(B) We must also enquire whether the person concerned has taken three due precautions against illusion.

(a) Has he feared to be deceived?

(b) Has he shown perfect frankness in counsel with advisers?

(c) Has he abstained from coveting revelations?

(C) There are also, according to Poulain, nine points upon which information should be obtained with regard to each private revelation.

(1) If it has been transmitted in writing, is there an absolutely authentic text of the record of it?

(2) Is the revelation capable of passing the test of coherence? (Poulain regards this test as that of coherence with the experience of the catholic church and with the undoubted pronouncement of history and science. Others may wish to impose a wider test here, but even that of the author in question has implications the full meaning of which one suspects that even Rome herself has hardly grasped.)

(3) Is the revelation in conformity with moral decency and charity?

(4) Is it useful for our eternal welfare? (God, remarks Poulain, does not go out of his way merely to satisfy curiosity.)

(5) Are the gravity and dignity of the detailed circumstances of the experience in keeping with THE DIVINE MAJESTY?

(6) What sentiments of peace or, on the other hand, of disquiet have accompanied the experience?

(7) What constructive result or new enterprise issues from the experience?

(8) Have these private revelations stood the test of time and scrutiny?

(9) Have subsequent events clearly shown that any new devotion issuing from the experience manifestly has the blessing of God?

Obviously no single one of the above tests can lead to certainty, and even a combination of several or of all can only give greater or lesser probability; while even if we take them in the form in which Rome accepts them, without reducing their number or altering their terms, their primary effect is drastically to reduce the credible elements in any piece of intuitional knowledge. Many will feel with me that the fore-closing of discussion here (as in the case of dogmatics) is futile, since Rome both in apologetics and in natural theology makes much of her appeal to reason. This appeal must be extended to all fields and nowhere excluded. Rome in fact is in the same case as others, and must needs apply her tests to the alleged revelations recorded in scripture. Having, however, said this much, it seems to me only gracious to acknowledge the help which in spite of its limitations Father Poulain's analysis gives us in scrutinising all sorts of individual experiences which claim the quality of givenness. We see from that analysis that it is no new or un-welcome idea to a great religious society that some of its members may be subject to illusions. The wonder is that any seers were ever believed, if modern scepticism be taken seriously.

I have dealt with Father Poulain at some length, partly because his work has been officially blessed by the Vatican and duly certificated, but also because it is obviously the result of very long and patient study. His analysis is so detailed in his book itself that it may easily repel some readers, and I have ventured here to abridge it; but from the point of view of religious psychology it is valuable, because of its detail and documentation. We can bear with him even when he records that those who practise the prayer of quiet must expect to suffer from cold feet!

I must now pass on to consider the position of these private intuitions from the point of view of mental and moral science. Assuming that on other grounds we find a balance of probability in favour of the belief that Self-Existent Being subsists, we may then ask: Is intuition, when coupled with great moral purity and spiritual earnestness, to be or not to be held capable of conveying intimations of purpose from the realm of Self-Existent Being? The psychologist with his methods of abstraction is reluctant, as we have seen, to give an affirmative answer. Apart from telepathy, clairvoyance, and lucky coincidence, all of which may account for some of the alleged intimations, the psychologist's reluctance is no doubt due to the technique of the visionary, with his ecstasies, his auditions and locutions, bodily images, and so on.

Curiously enough it is, I believe, Mr. Bernard Shaw who must get the credit of having rehabilitated Joan of Arc with the hard-headed English Protestant by saying in his preface that she was "a Galtonic visualiser." For any who may not be familiar with Francis Galton's pioneer work in the study of mental imagery a few words of explanation are desirable. Galton was a fellow of the Royal Society, most of whose work was done in the latter half of the nineteenth century, and who led the way in the accumulation of materials for the modern sciences of psychology and eugenics. In a volume of essays entitled "Enquiries into human faculty and its development" he devotes one section to a study of such imagery. Scientists who may read these introductory sentences with a little impatience must be good enough to remember that I am here writing for those who are not specialists in the subjects which Galton professed. He observed, he says, that there are a number of persons existing in all ages whose visual memory is so clear and sharp as to present mental pictures which may be scrutinised with nearly as much ease and prolonged attention as if they were material objects. His interest became aroused, and he was led to make a rather extensive enquiry into the mode of visual presentation in different persons so far as could be gathered from their respective statements. He therefore issued a number of questions to a variety of individuals on the homely topic of such a definite object as their mental picture of the breakfast table, at the time they sat down to it on the morning of the particular day when they were answering the questions.

"Before addressing yourself to any of the questions on the opposite page, think, and consider carefully the picture that rises before your mind's eye.

(1) Illumination. Is the image dim or fairly clear? Is its brightness comparable to that of the actual scene.

(2) Definition. Are all the objects pretty well defined at the same time, or is the place of sharpest definition at any one moment more contracted than it is in a real scene?

3. Colouring. Are the colours of the china, of the toast, bread-crust, mustard, meat, parsley, or whatever may have been on the table, quite distinct and natural?"

He began by questioning his friends in the scientific world, and to his astonishment he found that the great majority of those to whom he applied protested that mental imagery was unknown to them, and even supposed that those who affirmed they possessed it were romancing. They had in fact no more notion of visualising their recollection of a scene than a colour-blind man has of the nature of colour. On the other hand, Galton found that with persons whom he met in general society an entirely different disposition prevailed.   Many men and yet a larger number of women and many boys and girls declared that they habitually saw mental imagery, and that it was perfectly distinct to them and full of colour.   The more he pressed them, professing himself to be incredulous, the more obvious was the truth of their first assertions. They described their imagery in minute detail, and spoke with surprise of his apparent hesitation in accepting what they said.   He felt that he himself would have spoken exactly as they did, if he had been describing a scene that lay before his eyes in broad daylight to a blind man who persisted in doubting the reality of vision.   Reassured by this experience he returned to his enquiries among his scientific friends, and found scattered instances of what he had been seeking, though in by no means the same abundance as elsewhere; and he then classified and published his result in the case of a hundred Englishmen, nineteen of whom were fellows of the Royal Society, and twice or three times persons of distinction in various kinds of intellectual work.   The classification showed that one out of every sixteen of those accustomed to accurate speech described his mental imagery as perfectly clear and bright, in some such words as: "If I could draw I am sure I could draw perfectly from my mental image."   He notes that Blake, for example, was probably an adept at doing this, and that the power of playing blind-fold chess, in which a number of boards are visualised at a time, is greatly on the increase.   He described cases of persons who mentally read scores when playing a musical instrument, or, when they are making speeches, a manuscript which is not actually in front of them; while he records a few in which persons in an audience see mentally in print every word that is uttered by a preacher, attending to the visual equivalent rather than to the sound of the words. (The development of this faculty is obviously encouraged by the amusement commonly known to boy-scouts and others, from its occurrence in the pages of Kipling, as "Kim's game.") This visualising faculty, says Galton, is a natural gift, and like all natural gifts, has a tendency to be inherited, and he also thinks that the possession of it varies according to race. He regards the French, for example, as possessing the visualising faculty in a high degree. The peculiar ability they show in prearranging cere-monials and fêtes of all kinds, and their undoubted genius for tactics and strategy, show that they are able to foresee effects with unusual clearness. Their ingenuity in all technical contrivances is an additional testimony in the same direction, and so is their singular clearness of expression. Their phrase "figurez-vous," or "picture to yourself" seems to express their dominant mode of perception.

It is possible, though Galton does not refer to them, that he would have found the Semitic people to be strongly endowed with the visualising faculty. I do not think it would be difficult to prove that this is the explanation of much Hebrew prophetic imagery. A returned missionary from South India has also recorded cases in which converts spoke of having "*seen* Jesus Christ," when it was found that what they meant by these words was an interior or mental vision.   Galton declares that among uncivilised races one of the most gifted has proved to be that of the Bushmen in South Africa, and the well-known and proverbial bushman art of drawing animal figures seems to be associated with the ability to make mental images.   He also says that similar ability accompanied by great accuracy is shown by the Eskimo, one of whom, although a thorough barbarian in the accepted sense of the word, visualised in his memory a region over which he had at one time or another gone in his canoe, which comprised eleven hundred English miles, and then drew a chart of the region, which, on comparison, was found to be practically identical with the admiralty chart.   It is obvious that in these cases the visualisation chiefly concerned objects which had *already been seen* with the outward eye.   There appear, however, from Galton's record, to be a number of other phenomena which concern the association of ideas. Thus many people associate forms or pictures with certain numbers, or always see the numerals grouped in a particular pattern.   Others see colours associated with them, and sometimes these colours are regularly connected with a particular word or letter of the alphabet.   Thus of two sisters one always visualised the letter A as blue, while the other saw it as black. In another case a woman said that the word Wednesday always called up in her mind a kind of oval patch of a yellow emerald green, while Tuesday was grey, Thursday brownish red, and Friday a dull yellow.

In the course of his enquiries into visual memory Galton was greatly struck by the frequency of the

replies in which his informants described themselves
as "*subject to visions.*" These persons were sane and
healthy, but were subject notwithstanding to visual
presentations for which they could not account. He
adds that in a few cases they reached the level of
hallucinations. He regards this unexpected presence
of a visionary tendency among persons who form a
part of ordinary society to be suggestive and well
worthy of being put on record. The lowest order of
the phenomena which admit of being classed in this
way is that of the number-forms just mentioned.
These strange phenomena are almost incredible to the
vast majority of mankind, who would set them down
as fantastic nonsense; but to the rest they are both
vivid and familiar. The next sort of vision is the
instant association in some persons of colour with a
particular sound or word. A third is that which
connects a word with a visualised picture often due
to some association of ideas, as for instance when
Mrs. Haweis told Galton that she always thought of the
word "beast" as having a face like a gargoyle, which
was very likely due to her association of the word with
the passage in the Apocalypse in which the four com-
posite beasts are described. She went on to say,
however, that for some reason the word "green" also
had a gargoyle face with the addition of big teeth,
while the word "blue"

"blinks and looks silly and turns to the right, while the
word 'attention' has the eyes greatly turned to the left."

It seems important to draw a careful distinction
between (1) visions which are the mental reproduction
of things previously seen, (2) visions which reproduce

something which the recipient has not actually seen, but which exists somewhere else, and which by a process of telepathy or thought transference he is able to see, and (3) visions which are either fanciful creations of the mind or perceptions of objects actually existing which are believed to be present when they are not. Galton draws a distinction between what he calls induced visions and direct ones, and he thinks that they are often like dreams, patchworks built up of bits of recollections. These, of course, as in the case of dreams, will have a symbolic meaning, or rather the grouping will be symbolic. His statement that fasting, absence of sleep, and solitary musing are severally conducive to dreams are not only important, but alarming at first sight to those who believe in the visions of the saints, and who think that in this manner they are being explained away. It is worth considering whether the point at issue here is not whether all the visions induced by fasting are hallucinations, but whether moderate fasting, by enabling the system to overtake arrears of digestion, does not clarify the mind and produce a state of mental acuteness in which the powers of intuition and reason can attain maximum activity, and under such conditions in the case of persons who are naturally visualisers also produce sharply-defined visions; whereas excess of fasting by exhausting the nervous system will lead to unbalanced judgments and so possibly to hallucinations. (I am afraid we shall be compelled to write off as untrustworthy visions of this latter sort, as also those which are due to want of sleep.) It will be remembered that the Buddha caused a revolution in the practice

of Jhana, or meditation, by advising that it should be
practised not òn an entirely empty stomach but after
a moderate mid-day meal.   It is easy to dismiss the
visualisations and the voices (which by the way are
only another form of picturesque symbolic reproduc-
tions of mental experience) which are the product of
solitary musing, as equally untrustworthy.   But here
the type of test proposed by Poulain is obviously of
great importance.   Those who stand apart from the
crowd because they can see further through a brick
wall than most people must not invariably be dubbed
lunatics or neurotics.   Sometimes they really can see
further than ordinary folk, and their solitary concentration enables them to arrive at profound truths
which they then communicate in symbolic phraseology
supplied by the experiences of their daily life.   Often
they stumble because they are seeking to describe that
which is really beyond description with the symbols
at their disposal, and this leads less favoured intelli-
gences to treat them with injustice.   Visualisation,
however, even in its intensest form as ecstasy, is not
by any means a neuropathic phenomenon, for those
who experience it are often strong characters, origina-
tors of great projects, with strong wills and a high moral
ideal.   They do not covet honours, whereas the one
desire of hysterical subjects is to play a part before a
little circle of spectators.   The true saint, though he
may be a visualiser, need not necessarily be one, but
even if he is, that does not prove him a degenerate,
since he is on the contrary (so far as he is recognisably
a saint), full of typically heroic virtues, for the harmony
with Deity which is involved in the practice of religion

does not lead to a psychopathic condition but to heroism.

It is obvious that this somewhat lengthy exposition of Galton's researches only covers the case of persons who express their intuition in the form of a bodily image. It does not account for the intuition itself, or for the existence of alleged interior locutions. Yet I think the Galtonic principle may be carried further to include these as well. A rapid synthetic mental process, or (if such be allowed possible), an immediate perception or "opening,"[1] in which the recipient is passive or neutral rather than active or engaged in research, may be recorded and communicated to others in a picturesque piece of verbal symbolism.

But such verbal symbolism need not invalidate the truth of what has been received. To say "Thus hath the Lord shewed me" need not involve the speaker in self-deception or fraud any more than to say "I have had an intuition." Interpretative prophecy, or a record of guidance given, may truthfully employ either phrase.

It is also apparently unnecessary for the person who ultimately develops visualising tendencies to be naturally endowed with them, for Saint Teresa records that she found it almost impossible to picture scenes to herself in meditation, which would hardly have been the case if she had been a visualiser by nature. Yet at a later period in her life she records that after a time of psychic distress an awareness came to her which was not with the eyes of the body but which

[1] George Fox's term.

carried with it intense certitude. Her words are important because of the admission.

"At the end of two years spent in prayer by myself and others for this end, namely, that our Lord would either lead me by another way, or show the truth of this—for now the locutions of our Lord were extremely frequent—this happened to me. I was in prayer one day—it was the feast of the glorious St. Peter—when I saw Christ close by me, or, to speak more correctly, felt Him; for I saw nothing with the eyes of the body, nothing with the eyes of the soul. He seemed to me to be close beside me; and I saw, too, as I believe, that it was He who was speaking to me. As I was utterly ignorant that such a vision was possible, I was extremely afraid at first, and did nothing but weep; however, when He spoke to me but one word to reassure me, I recovered myself, and was, as usual, calm and comforted, without any fear whatever. Jesus Christ seemed to be by my side continually, and, as the vision was not imaginary, I saw no form; but I had a most distinct feeling that He was always on my right hand, a witness of all I did; and never at any time, if I was but slightly recollected, or not too much distracted, could I be ignorant of His near presence. I went at once to my confessor in great distress, to tell him of this. He asked in what form I saw our Lord. I told him I saw no form. He then said: 'How did you know that it was Christ?' I replied that I did not know how I knew it; but I could not help knowing that He was close beside me . . . there are no words whereby to explain—at least, none for us women, who know so little; learned men can explain it better."

This was plainly what is called an intellectual vision, and was not the same as "imaginary vision," of which Mrs. Stuart Moore[1] writes:—

[1] Better known as Evelyn Underhill. Her book *Mysticism* (1904) is now in a fourth edition.

"Imaginary vision is the spontaneous and automatic activity of a power which all artists, all imaginative people possess. So far as the machinery employed in it is concerned there is little real difference except in degree between Wordsworth's—

". . . when on my couch I lie
In vacant or in pensive mood,
They flash upon that inward eye
Which is the bliss of solitude;
And then my heart with pleasure fills,
And dances with the daffodils."

And the descriptions given by Henry Suso of the dancing angels, who 'though they leapt very high in the dance did so without any lack of gracefulness.' Both are admirable examples of passive imaginary vision: though in the first case the visionary is aware that the picture seen is supplied by memory, whilst in the second it arises spontaneously like a dream from the subliminal region, and contains elements which may be attributed to love, belief, and direct intuition of proof. Such passive imaginary vision—spontaneous mental pictures at which the self looks but in the action of which it does not participate—takes in the mystics two main forms; (a) purely symbolic, (b) personal."

Mrs. Moore goes on to describe the characteristics of these two forms of vision. In the first there is no mental deception, and the self is aware all the time that what it is seeing is only truth under an image. In the second the contact of the soul with the absolute Life is so swift and dazzling that although the imagery by which it is accompanied is just as much symbolic as in the first place it is so vivid that it is not always recognised as symbolic. In other words the symbolism in the former case is merely instructive, in the latter, like a sacrament, it is dynamic in that it conveys grace.[1] As Delacroix says:—

"The immanent God, formless, but capable of assuming all forms, expresses Himself in vision as He had expressed Himself in words."

And Mrs. Moore adds the comment:—

"Certainty and joy are always felt by the self which experiences the vision. It is as it were a love letter received by the ardent soul: which brings with it the very fragrance of personality, along with the sign-manual of the beloved."

A really serious objection meets us, of course, from those who would deny the intuitive attainment of any religious knowledge; and it needs careful examination. If no intuitive perception of anything ever occurs, then obviously there can be no intuitive perception of religious truth. Moreover, even if that occurs which is called intuitive and immediate, but is only thought to be so, and is in reality the product of actual mediations and synthetic mental operations of which we are unaware, then that occurrence is improperly labelled, and must be taken as only a special and unusual case of inferential knowledge, and not as something which is in a different class altogether. In other words, we have ' to consider whether all immediacy is " of that spurious kind which consists in unawareness of actual mediations and of

[1] The reader is invited to study again in the light of the above reflections the visions recorded in the Bible, not only those of the Hebrew prophets, but also those of the Risen and Ascended Christ, and still further the visions recorded in the Book of Revelation.

acquired facility in synthesis and deduction,"[1] or whether there can be a genuine immediacy in which apprehension is direct. The truth, as has been pointed out, is that no intuition can be literally instantaneous. Even a "flash" must be of *some* duration, and there may be some processes which are too rapid for their stages to be introspectively differentiated, yet which are real processes. Truths which seem self-evident to an expert or even to a civilised person are not self-evident to the amateur or to the savage.

The question thus becomes one of interpretation, and of preconceived ideas. Are we or are we not forbidden to say that any process whether telescoped or non-mediated can be "*given*"? In other words, does God ever give knowledge except through the reasoning faculties? If we answer "yes," may we use that knowledge as an argument for His existence, or must we say that we should not know that it came from Him if we had not already decided on other grounds that He did exist? Or is it the case that "showings" and "revelations" have led some of us to look around for explanations, so that reasoning followed them and did not precede them, and that a direct experience made us say "There must be God, I will see whether reason confirms this experience," and that then but only then the theistic hypothesis seemed to be a plausible construction out of inferential data?

The question at issue is thus not (1) Is intuition a more valuable source of information than intelligent reasoning? but (2) Is it a different one? Obviously, if we are seeking evidence, it makes all the difference

[1] Tennant, Tarner Lectures.

whether an item described as B is really B or only a form of A. If it is the latter it can add nothing new to our total evidence; but if it is what it appears to be, B and not A, and if A and B are fundamentally different classes then plainly we have two distinct sorts of evidence instead of one.

Now Bergson's theory of intuition is perfectly clear and understandable. It stresses immediacy as a distinct source of knowledge, and maintains that what in animals appears as instinct in human beings is raised to a higher power, functioning with delicate accuracy, and giving not only more rapid results than reason, but also results which anticipate the findings arrived at by slower and more pedestrian methods. It has, however, been freely criticised, and is to-day less fashionable than twenty-five years ago. Nevertheless we have to recognise that both Höffding and Sorley, two of Bergson's most eminent critics, while they do not entirely agree with him, agree with one another in accepting intuition of some kind as a *distinct* source of knowledge. Thus Höffding[1] points out that Bergson does not sufficiently distinguish between the intuition which is the result of all psychical activity and the intuition which is "the summit and conclusion of the work of thought." The former, exemplified in sensation, memory, and imagination is what Höffding calls concrete intuition. The latter, exemplified by the comprehensive class in which a total scheme of thought is grasped, he calls synthetic intuition. Sorley similarly says that Bergson does not sufficiently distinguish between (1) the immediate knowledge

[1] *History of European Philosophy.*

of which we have sense-perception, and the consciousness of our own inner life, and (2) the synoptic
views of reality by which we get wholes like one's
self or other selves, or a world-view.

It is a commonplace that any analysis of knowledge
has to make a place for direct perception. Thus
William James in his *Principles of Psychology*, writes:

"There are two kinds of knowledge broadly and
practically distinguishable; we may call them respectively *knowledge of acquaintance* and *knowledge-about*.
Most languages express the distinction thus: γνῶναι,
εἰδέναι; noscere, scire; kennen, wissen; connaître,
savoir . . . I know the colour blue when I see it and the
flavour of a pear when I taste it . . . but *about* the inner
nature of these facts or what makes them what they
are I can say nothing at all. I cannot impart acquaintance with them to anyone who has not already
made it himself. I cannot describe them, make a
blind man guess what blue is like, or tell a philosopher
in just what respect distance is just what it is, and
differs from other forms of relation. At most I can
say to my friends, Go to certain places and act in
certain ways and these objects will probably come."
And Oman, distinguishing four types of knowing:
(*a*) awareness, (*b*) apprehension, (*c*) comprehension,
(*d*) explanation, shows that (*a*) and (*b*) are plainly
matters of direct perception though in (*b*) the field is
narrower than in (*a*) while (*c*) and (*d*) introduce the
element of *considering*.

The point at issue therefore seems to be: "Since
immediacy is incapable of being ruled out, can Deity
be and is He the object of *direct* perception, as well as

an explanatory Principle deduced from efforts to
comprehend the whole as well as the details of the
field of vision?" Those who answer "No" must
logically exclude the practices of religious devotion
such as direct prayer and direct seeking for guidance,
since these depend entirely upon the assumption that
Deity is directly *en rapport* with the devout. The
situation thus stated is seen to be intolerable, since
it violates too large a mass of sober experience, and
leaves us with the absurdity that if Deity *is*, in the
sense of being discoverable by induction, He has
no intercourse at all with the spirit of man, but
invariably leaves His messages to be inferred in a
roundabout way.

There seems to be some confusion in the use of terms.
The word mysticism is probably too hard-worked and
is in danger of being used as the equivalent of (*a*) direct
perception, (*b*) prophetic interpretative insight, (*c*) pan-
sacramentalism, (*d*) the *via negativa*, which is "a
technique of withdrawing desire by means of asceticism
away from the Natural; of preventing the senses from
witnessing to it by excluding all images of sense;
and then by suppressing all thinking even as con-
templation, of passing into . . . ecstatic union with
the One, and passive reception of the Divine."

Now it cannot usefully mean all these things; and
it were better perhaps to avoid employing it altogether
rather than risk confusion and misunderstanding.
Thus one American writer in order to clear the issue
distinguishes between positive and negative mysticism,
meaning by the latter the *via negativa*. But positive
mysticism must be further subdivided into the introvert

or silent and the extravert or prophetic. There is a vital difference, as we have seen, between these, which bids fair to become increaingly important in future religious thought. A nature-mystic or pan-sacramentalist and a catholic mystic (who is sometimes a hepta-sacramentalist) may neither of them exercise or possess the gift of interpretative prophecy. On the other hand the prophet can have nothing to proclaim unless something has been shown to him through nature or through reflection upon the course of events.

It appears then that in spite of (or perhaps because of) all the verbal or pictorial imagery of the prophets and seers, there is a corpus of truth intuitively perceived by them which is capable of being tested and sifted from the error with which it is mixed; and that when it has been sifted out we find that it consists (a) in the stretching forward in expectation to a discrimination of truth of which the reason within most persons only becomes aware by using more pedestrian methods, (b) in the intuitive interpretation of that which is manifested to us whether as *physical world*, or as *historical sequence*, so that in the slow and sometimes faltering progress of rational research we gradually realise in sober fact inch by inch that to which our seers have stretched forward in expectant anticipation, and indeed have already grasped intuitively, (c) in the extrapolation of the readings which reason provides.

REVELATION

We naturally pass at this point to that important topic, the relation of discovery to revelation. Has

there ever been or is there such a thing as the latter?
Now it must first be pointed out that revelation in
the sense of responsiveness is a fact which we may
and do perceive in more ways than one. A willingness
to be known may manifest itself to reason quite as
as much as to intuition, and there is thus no case for
distinguishing between the undoubted revelations
made to scientists who discover the constitution and
course of Nature, and the equally undoubted revelations
of the Will and character of Deity which are derived
from the prophetic vision, which is seldom wholly
interior, but is closely connected with interpretations
of the course of nature and of external events, since
these speak "rememberable things" to the seer who
observes them. In one sense discovery and revelation
are the obverse and reverse of a single object, the
god-ward and the man-ward aspects of the same
process. In common parlance, however, we reserve
the word revelation for that in which the initiative
of Deity bulks more largely than the enterprise of
man. It is that which is released or given, and the
greater the gift or release the greater the revelation.
We have seen that what is described as the prophetic
consciousness is a series of special instances of intuitive
knowledge of an exceptionally high order, which the
recipients instead of keeping to themselves felt
impelled to deliver to others. A brief consideration
of the consciousness of the greater Hebrew prophets
should be sufficient to establish this.

It is also obvious to the historical student that the
consciousness of Jesus of Nazareth was of the same
type. The problem to be solved concerns the relation

of the prophets and Jesus to other religious seers.
Was their intuitive and interpretative knowledge of a
different order? Was it different in kind or only in
degree? Are we to say that there was a break between
the prophets and other seers? and again a break
between the prophets and Jesus? Our forefathers
were accustomed to answer these questions in the
affirmative, and to draw a sharp distinction between
natural and revealed religion, and further to treat
revelation as beginning with the Hebrew prophets,
who prepared the way for the coming of a supreme
and final revelation. Now it will be of little avail
to sweep aside the assertions of our forefathers as
invalid. Their description of the facts may be ob-
jectionable to an age which believes in the principle
of continuity as permeating the cosmic process, and
dislikes the idea of breaks in the chain of events, for
this dislike is not mere prejudice, though it leads
thinkers sometimes into the snare of treating indisputable facts with unfairness. In this particular
case our forefathers were perfectly correct in recognising
a vast qualitative distinction as existing between, let
us say, the teaching of Deutero-Isaish and the teachings
of primitive polytheism, and again between the
teaching of Deutero-Isaiah and that of Jesus.[1] The
rejection of their explanation in no way justifies anyone
in ignoring indisputable facts. It will be legitimate
to say that all discovery is due to revelation, and that
the apprehension of revelation is discovery; but we

[1] Though it must be granted that ethical ideas formerly supposed
confined to Hebrew prophecy are discoverable in Sumerian and
Egyptian literature, and that even Jesus had features in common
with His contemporaries.

need not for that reason treat all discoveries as of equal
importance, nor all revelations as possessing equal
intensity. Life is not a dead-level, either from the
point of view of geography or history, and although
we may now be able to trace religion back to its
primitive origin and to show that in the course of its
development there is no real gap between natural
and revealed religion, since all knowledge is in some
sense revelation, this need not and does not make any
serious difference to our belief that in the Hebrew
prophetic consciousness we have an instance of a
discontinuous development of great magnitude in the
intuitive apprehension of knowledge, and also a still
greater discontinuity in the emergence of the person
of the historical Jesus. But discontinuities do not
necessarily involve spatial intrusions of alien elements.
We cannot accept the geometrical pictures of revelation
as a tangent almost but not quite touching a circle,
nor have we any need to do so. Revelation may be
perfectly genuine and yet part of the order of nature,
an arrangement (with special additions) of what
already exists in a fragmentary, sporadic, or disjointed
manner, and the revelation of Jesus is not mere verbal
prophetic utterance, but *word in life*, the message
conveyed not merely in ecstatic utterance but in a
Career. Perhaps, when all is said and done, it is the
degree of initiative on the one side or the other which
determines whether an event is to be properly described
as discovery or as revelation. The Christian Gospel
certainly puts forth its claim on the ground that it is
in the main the story of something which is pre-
dominantly an Act of God.

Corrective note to "Revelation."

It will be seen that I differ here considerably from Barth. I fully recognise that *mere* searching cannot find out Deity, unless it is accompanied by reverent humility, and a sense of one's own limitations and imperfections, with the effort to purify and amend; unless also there is that element of responsiveness or willingness to be known, which is ready to reward our search. But such responsiveness plainly has its degrees, and sometimes becomes an initiative to which *we* have to respond. This and this only is what Barth is prepared to call Revelation, and he therefore parts company from such English thinkers as Prof. Gwatkin and James Maurice Wilson, because he holds that the modernist is much too optimistic about human faculty. The latter is not merely in a wounded condition, but is in such a state of total depravity that it cannot of itself discover even as much as natural theology (here Barth shows how his anthropology differs from that of the Roman Catholics to whom in his affirmation of the Fall he seems to draw near; but the approximation is apparent rather than real, because Lutheran and Reformed theology have always taught that the Fall was from Nature into Corruption; whereas Roman Catholic theology holds that it involves a deprivation of Supernature, leaving man in Nature, but bereft of the power to rise into Supernature without the aid of grace.)

Now my emphasis upon sin is different from Barth's. Hence I allow more for the element of human initiative, met by Divine responsiveness. But I am quite ready to recognise degrees of Divine initiative ($\pi o \lambda u \mu \epsilon \rho \hat{\omega} s$ $\kappa a \grave{\iota}$ $\pi o \lambda u \tau \rho \acute{o} \pi \omega s$) culminating in the Revelation through Jesus. What I fail to see is how Barth establishes, except by emphatic reiteration, the Absoluteness and Finality of this crowning Revelation—its once-for-all-ness. Merely to assert it is no proof; and without some kind of philosophy

PHILLIPS MEMORIAL
LIBRARY
PROVIDENCE COLLEGE

of religion I do not see how we can get any probability, (complete proof is of course impossible).

Further, for some curious reason Barth does not seem to feel the sense of the New Revelation given to us through the natural sciences, of which so much is made in this country. Possibly the university faculties are more divided than in England (they have no college high-tables in Germany, and dons do not meet socially so much) and theology is more departmentalised. Possibly also there was not the same exhilaration in Germany over scientific research as we felt in post-war Cambridge. The atom had been split here, not in Bonn, and even Darwin was a Cambridge man; while the popularisation of the new cosmogonies has been due to local effort. Hence our difference of outlook from that of the Reformed Churches of the continent. A supremely great Word of God doubtless comes to us *in* and through the Bible. But we live in a world which rightly or wrongly we feel to be full of Words of God. The earth and the common face of nature, and the patient researches of truth-seekers, indeed yield and speak to us rememberable things. We may exaggerate the importance of these new words, but it is idle to pretend that they are not for many honest and reverent persons a good deal more important than what Barth calls "Wort Gottes," still more so because Barth will insist upon the fallenness of humanity, and this for the anthropologist is a hard saying, and leads him to suspect that the theologian is here guilty of rationalisation, and is trying to keep the old terminology with a new meaning, for the sake of loyalty to the past.

But there is a still greater difference between Barth and the modern doctrine of Revelation as formulated by British theologians. For many years we have been accustomed to the idea of *progressive* revelation, proceeding *not necessarily* in a mechanically even manner but by *measure*, and certainly not all at once. Barth contradicts this with the blunt assertion that it is *not* the belief which lies behind the Bible. Here we have no idea of evolution, not even of transilience or discontinuous progress, but of divers actions in each of which every time the *whole* Deity is revealed. This contradiction is perhaps not so evident as it seems, since Barth also concedes that in the experiences of those who witness the Revelation a measure of development does occur, and so he gives back some of what he had taken away. But British theology feels itself on safer ground in not treating the Bible in two different ways. If the Bible does not give us the idea of progressive revelation, treated as a collection of documents, there are many other ideas about the world given to us by it which we now know not to be true, and there is no reason for accepting it as authoritative in the one case rather than in the other. The fact remains that if we interpret this collection of documents "like any other collection" we get a consistent picture of human discovery and Divine responsiveness, plus an element of Divine initiative, the whole forming a graduated scheme with its pivotal point in the past, yet marching on into the future. Granted the scientific investigator is apt to show undue contempt for the idea of Revelation, it is equally possible for thinkers like Barth to be too much in a department of life to do justice to the scientist. Of course Julian Huxley almost delivers the game into Barth's hands when he describes religion without revelation as a purely human activity, because this· is just what Barth himself says, and wants his opponents to admit that it is. As we see, however, the scientists go on to retort that there is no reason for supposing the revelation of which Barth speaks to be more than the objectification of human desires, and they would regard him as a pathetically industrious professor constructing a system upon the basis of an inherited loyalty to biblical Protestantism, a loyalty of the psychological basis of which he is apparently unaware. Now apart from our single method of organising and reflecting upon experience we can have no means of judging the validity of an alleged revelation. It is, therefore, futile to exclude the scientific approach to religion and to treat it as irrelevant, even though it may only yield a good working hypothesis instead of a "Deus dixit." After all, what wrong is there in seeking a pragmatic verification that God has spoken, by taking "Deus dixit" as a hypothesis, rather than shouting "Deus dixit" without being able to give any reason for the proclamation?

I hope, however, that no one will suppose that in this treatise discovery and willingness to be known are merely equated with Divine initiative or revelation. Plainly in all things *God comes first*, and His self-expressive activity is *prior* to all his creatures, and so to their discovery of Him and His ways. Without God, discovery of God would be impossible, and it is only through His gift to us of our wits that we are able to experience Him at all. We have nothing that we have not received. Nevertheless, from the human standpoint God's priority means nothing to us until we have experienced it. Hence discovery must be set over against responsiveness, and even against the special initiative which we call the self-revelation of character by God.

CHRISTIAN EXPERIENCE

It has been said that Christianity is essentially an experimental religion, or perhaps we should say religion whose main defence is to be found in experiment. A recent writer upon ethics refers to the disparagement of reason which has accompanied the progress of Christianity.[1] This, of course, is an

[1] Stephen Ward, *A History of Ethics*. (Oxford Univ. Press.)

unfriendly way of stating the case. Yet it is certainly
true that the legacy which the Christian movement
inherited from the prophets of Israel was different
from that inherited by the non-Christian world from
the philosophers of antiquity. Hence Christians have
tended to say: "Believe in what we tell you, because
we have it on the authority not of those who have
sat down and worked it out, but on the authority of
those who have received it as in a flash from the mind
of God Himself. Trust their experience and you will
come to find that they have not been deceived. He
that doeth the truth shall know of the doctrine. Make
the experiment and you will come to be convinced
that the Christian reading of life is correct." Now in
regard to these allegations it may be asked: "If these
experiments succeed, can they convince anyone in
whom they have so far not succeeded?" This question,
moreover, assumes the possibility that in certain cases
the experiment may have been found to fail, and this
raises the further question: "Since there are obviously
cases in which sincere persons have made experiments
on the basis of Christian belief and have met with
disappointment, does this involve either its inadequacy
or its error?" To this it may be replied that the
experiment of Christian living has so often succeeded,
that when an alleged Christian experiment fails it is
fair to assume either that the experimenter has done
something to hinder its success, or that it was the wrong
form of experiment and ought never to have been tried.
The right form of Christian experiment must always
include the possibility of the cross. No one has any
right to expect to be able to evade the possibility of

his own Calvary; but since the original experience of the first Calvary has been seen to have issued in ultimate triumph, any subsequent identification with the totality of that experience must end in similar triumph. Thus the *right* Christian experiment can never fail, because it involves complete identification with the life of the Lord, and so produces an inward state of harmony, which, though it may suffer and agonise can never be dislodged from its conviction of optimism about ultimate issues.

We may distinguish between (1) experiences which interpret external happenings and discern their underlying meaning as signs of Divine purpose and activity, and (2) wholly internal experiences. Of the former type are those interpretations of the course of history which display exceptional insight: of the latter are the "messages to conscience" which have sometimes guided individuals to momentous actions.

Christian experience means, of course, the experience of lives lived in harmony with Deity christianly conceived. "Thus hath the Lord dealt with me" is their message. It is a story of religious intimacy which hardly exists outside Christianity save in some of the Psalms and in the Bhakti literature of India: yet it is far from being an intense pantheistic mysticism. God and the soul are still two separate entities, and probably to many simple Jesuolatrous Christians, Jesus Christ has been so much a separate being from God the Father that the fellowship and intimacy have been with Him rather than with the latter. Christian experience is thus (1) a Christian form of general prophetic experience, in which the course of events is

interpreted as being under the guidance or control of
Deity or as manifesting His Initiative, (2) a mystical
inward experience in which the individual habitually
lives ἐν Χριστῷ and is united to Deity through that
identification of self with Christ.   This is the experience
of the Christian saints, and it is the source of their
unparalleled creative energy and strength of character.
The claim is made that this is a higher form of mysticism than the self-abandoning pantheistic mysticism
of the East.   The claim is also made that all forms of
Christian experience issue in the highest form of
personal religion which this planet produces.

The question will of course be asked whether such a
credal experiment is merely automatic in its effect, and
succeeds equally well, no matter whether what is
believed in is true or not.

To this the answer must be that of course all credal
experiments partially succeed, if only because an
organised and unified personality is always better than
a disorganised one.   Hence the experiment of agnosti-
cism or of even downright atheism will in some measure
succeed, (as it certainly has succeeded), if it can be
made with enough heartiness.   The measure of
satisfaction both for the individual and the race is,
however, proportionate to the measure of intellectual
truth which the system contains.   Deity, grace, and
the life that is worth while—these are the ingredients
of all organised human existence.   Militant atheism
satisfies the desire for an organised life at the price of
starving or perverting it, or of devoting its energies
to limited and ultimately unsatisfying ends.   Some
systems ignore one or more of the three ingredients,

others exaggerate one at the expense of the others. The claim may justly be set forward that so far in actual practice what is known as Christian theism has shown the greatest capacity of any complex of credenda for satisfying the varied needs (not wants) of mankind. This is not, of course, the same as to say that no other system can or will ever arise more capable of performing that function. That is to make a very large assumption, though an assumption which has not only been made, but successfully defended. No clearer antithesis has ever been stated than that if Self-existent Being be some day shown to be qualitatively better than as shown in the character of Jesus, then that Being will deserve the greater adoration. If, on the other hand, Self-existent Being is less good than in the character of Jesus, we are left face to face with the grave intellectual difficulty that the latter is qualitatively superior to the Source which produced it.

SENSE OF SIN: GRACE: AND CONVERSION

There are three elements in human nature which in effect produce what is grouped together in religion under the term "sin." These are (1) failure to rise, (2) decline from a higher level, and (3) actual perversion.

Let us here enlarge a little upon the general ideal of "sin," and also explain what is meant by the term "grace," since it has been asserted that the latter is the most distinctive idea which is present in the developed form of Christianity.

1. *Sin*

Man is in substance potentially good, as good as any other raw material of the universe. This involves

a somewhat different view from that taught by theologians a hundred years ago, and needs to be justified.
The primitive cosmogony in Genesis certainly seems to
suggest that the whole of creation, including mankind,
was held by God to be very good, until at a definite
stage mankind tripped and fell, and a new element,
evil, suddenly and discontinuously appeared. The
studies of biologists compel us to modify our interpretation of this ancient myth and to treat it less
literally, while retaining its religious value. Evil
appears in our universe less as a sudden discontinuity
than as an element tending to produce a discontinuity,
which is present in different forms everywhere, and not
confined to the human species. Pure descriptive biology cannot record it as "Sin," since to do so involves
a moral judgment of value, the introduction of which
would mar the purity of scientific abstraction. Nevertheless, biology itself finds a difficulty in ignoring
qualitative ideas, so that we find even descriptive
biologists using such phrases as shadows, disharmonies,
progress, degeneration, and in one case a pair of words
"anabolic" and "katabolic," denoting two opposite
tendencies in development. The fact is that, without
some act of faith as to the direction in which the
arrow is pointing, descriptive biology is helpless. It
may find afterwards that it has been reading the
relation to one another of the things which it studies
backwards or upside down; but it has to read them in
some way or other. It cannot be content to take them
merely as isolated and meaningless symbols. Regarded however in this way, the phenomena of life do
seem to show elements which may be called respectively

"good" and "bad," and those in particular which in human beings are variously described as ugly, vicious, criminal, or sinful are plainly of the same quality as (though possibly different in degree and variety from) those which in other parts of the universe we call katabolic, parasitic, pathological, degenerate, anti-social, morbid, diseased or again merely ugly. The existence of these elements is so indisputable, that as a means of accounting for the universality of the supposed "taint" the theory has even been advanced of the premundane corruption of the world-soul, or even of creative evolution as involving a "fall" from eternity into time. The objection to this is that it seems to involve not only an assumption for which there is no evidence, but also the idea of an adverse element introduced from somewhere else, and this only postpones the solution of the problem, since we have to enquire how that element from somewhere else itself became what is called "evil"; in addition to which the nature of the super-universe excludes the idea of a "somewhere else." Whatever arises must take its form within the super-universe. There is no "outside" from which it can be introduced. It seems better therefore to regard the adverse element (call it "katabolic" or whatever else you like) as emerging temporarily within the continuum of the super-universe as the result of a certain capacity for freedom which that process itself contains. Such an explanation will be found to give the best sense, and until a better one comes along, it seems wise to adopt it. With the details of the katabolic element in that part of the universe which lies outside the human species we are not here occupied, but we confine ourselves to a consideration of its significance so far as man is concerned. Broadly speaking we may say that the failure to see mankind steadily and as a whole has led to two serious misjudgments as to its character. The conception of human goodness has been most emphasised in the ethical system of the Chinese Confucius. So strongly did he insist upon it that it has formed the natural outlook of the average Chinaman almost ever since. Thus an Englishman was once told by a Chinese parent not to punish his son (who was attending the Englishman's school) because such punishment would disturb the boy's sense of self-respect and make him lose confidence in his own goodness. The label Confucian, is however, no more to be confined to a particular doctrine of human nature which occurs in China than the label Acheulean to a particular artefact found at the type-station of St. Acheul. The type, if real, may occur anywhere, and may find expression even in the leading article of a popular Anglo-Saxon newspaper.[1] In like fashion we may without serious harm label as Augustinian the opposite view of human nature, always providing that its area of distribution be not limited to the Mediterranean countries.

It is well-expressed in the sixth chapter of the Westminster Confession, where we read: "Our first parents . . . being the root of all mankind, . . . the corrupted nature (was) conveyed to all their posterity descending from them by ordinary generation. From

[1] Or in such a saying as "Don't undervalue yourself. Other people will do that for you."

this original corruption, whereby we are utterly indisposed, disabled, and made opposite to all good, and wholly inclined to all evil, do proceed all actual transgressions."

A whole group of phrases (comprising conviction of sin, sense of guilt, being under the curse, having one's sin covered, expiation, atonement, imputed righteousness, justification), seems to be derived not merely from the world of the law-courts, but also from the intensity of feeling which is connected with the possession of what is called the twice-born temperament. Whatever explanation this temperament may receive from the hands of psychology, its claims are imperious, and it has always played a very large, and, as some wou'd think, a disproportionate part in the story of religion, on account of its driving power.

That the fear of God in many different senses has been a prominent element in the religion of the past can scarcely be denied, and in its more refined forms has taken the shape of an intense consciousness of moral delinquency. Such a consciousness is familiar from the descriptions given of it in the writings of St. Augustine, Luther, Bunyan, and others. It has often been the avowed aim and the accepted task of mission preachers to try to bring about this so-called conviction of sin. That in many cases they are right in breaking up self-complacency and causing men to see themselves as they really are may be readily admitted. At the same time psychopathologists know very well that there is a form of nervous malady known as scrupulosity which may attack persons of a neurotic temperament, or persons (and even communities) when they are

passing through an unstable period of life, and that
this may lead them not only to exaggerate the heinous-
ness of their offences, but also to become greatly
preoccupied with fears for their own safety, and
much depressed at the thought of their unworthiness
in the sight of God.

In view of the frequent assertions made on the one
hand that in no sense can the fall of man be salvaged
as an article of belief, and the equally violent assertions
on the other side that man is essentially fallen, and
that the first three chapters of Genesis contain real and
true history, "though doubtless written in a popular
and non-scientific manner"—in which latter assertion
both Catholics and the post-war school of Protestants
appear to unite—it seems advisable to state once and
for all a doctrine of man which adheres strictly to
observed fact, and at the same time preserves the sense
of guilt, upon which so much stress is laid in evangelical
and especially in Lutheran theology. It must be
clearly recognised that there is not a shred of evidence
for man having ever existed in an actually supernatural
state of original righteousness from which he
deteriorated. Man, as he emerges, exhibits a higher
capacity for autonomy and a larger element of
indeterminacy than creatures below him in the scale of
development. Yet he is not wholly and perfectly
free, and his lack of complete freedom is due not
merely to the survival within him of automatic
elements, but to his actual failures to progress, and to
wilful departures from the main track of normal
upward development, both of which not infrequently
tend to become habitual, and so enslave and hamper

him.   This is the true element in the Lutheran concept
of *servum arbitrium*, and its meaning will be all the
clearer if we bear in mind that according to Luther, only
Deity possesses *liberum arbitrium* in full completeness.
(It will be observed that this is a parallel to the
off-repeated statement that only Deity is fully and
completely personal.) It follows that creation, in
whatever sense it be described or interpreted, may not
inaptly be termed (in picturesque language) a potential
fall.   Judged scientifically, however, such language is
misleading, because it springs from a one-sided view.
We might with equal justice speak of creation as a
potential rise.   The assured facts about mankind are
a pathetic mixture of progress and failure, of departure
and fruitfulness, and we cannot regard it as proven
that, whatever may happen individually or locally,
mankind taken as a whole shows signs of moving
permanently further and further away from a goal of
spiritual perfection, nor is this a necessary postulate
for theology.

    At the same time it needs to be recognised that man's
capacity for free action, so far as it exists, is not of his
own manufacture, but a divine gift, and therefore,
although now his own and completely in his hands,
nevertheless represents the action of Deity, as it were
at one remove.   Through this element of freedom the
divine activity is directed, released, inhibited, or per-
verted in the world, so that it is possible to agree with
Spinoza when he declares that even the wicked do in
their fashion the will of God, though they are not on
that account in any way comparable to the good.
It is, therefore, not a Pelagian error to admit that in

all our good actions the prime element must be an
act of ours, so long as we acknowledge that that
act consists in a decision of obedience (what
Lutheran theologians describe as "Entscheidung" or
"Gehorsam") and not in the special activities
themselves, which, without the preliminary motivation,
will even at their best prove to be *splendida vitia*,
magnificent pieces of wilfulness.

We are now in a position to evaluate the phrase
"justification by faith," commonly (and rightly)
regarded as the corner-stone of reformed Christianity.
The thought of justification or acquittal and the desire
for it spring plainly from a group of persons who, when
confronted with the problems of life, put the question:
"What is going to happen to me?" The question implies rather more than curiosity—*i.e.* numinous uneasiness, and especially a misgiving that one is somehow
or other guilty of an improper reaction towards reality.
There is a resultant sense of helplessness as though the
ground were shaking under one's feet, and a desire for
security. On the assumption that man's capacity for
free action is a divine gift (Deity, as it were, at one
remove), and that all life is thus in some sense the
spirit of God in action, it seems that the word "faith" or
"trust," if taken as the equivalent of "decision," must
be understood in an active rather than in a passive sense.

That there is something in the idea of the Fall which
is more than the mere recognition of the occurrence of
a historical event is eloquently maintained by certain
continental Protestant theologians. Thus it is said
that in that totality of phenomena which we call "the
world" we see a vital impulse, which, although it may

have been imparted by God to all life through creation, is now nevertheless in definite opposition, negatively or positively, to the Will of God. "As seen in man, this will to live, this urgent desire of the creature for life is an effort of some sort to increase the size, the height, the length, of our self, our little ego. Even our higher spiritual life becomes in some form either positively or negatively the struggle for existence; and it is maintained that in such a setting out of the ego to live out its nature and to unfold itself, Adam, that is to say mankind, has become guilty, has transgressed the law and has become evil, so that its finest and most earnest and ever so well-meant accomplishments will always bear the stamp of this great vital urge."[1]

Even the highest and most intimate Christian religious impulses are thus capable of being brought to this biological denominator, and of being understood as a life-activity alongside of others, and equally questionable, while guilt and transitoriness are regarded as the main characteristics of even our best deeds. The one immediate criticism of such an estimate of human activity is that, however true it may or may not prove to be, to associate it with the word "Fall" (which has a definite *historical* content) is in the highest degree misleading. Disgrace, failure, departure, may be proper terms, but "Fall" must mean a descent from a place A to a lower place B; and even if the individual be situated at B, neither a movement from B to a still lower place C instead of a rise to A, nor a failure to

[1] Karl Barth, *Addresses on the Christian Life.*

move from B to a point A never hitherto reached, can merit the use of such a term.[1]

Passing on, however, from this criticism, the larger question remains: Is such an estimate, even so modified, a correct one? The answer to this will depend on an examination of the process by which it is reached.

It is surely idle to deny that the estimate is the two-fold product of a subjective mental disquietude, which may be produced (1) either by internal conflict or by external disasters, and (2) by the inherited respect for St. Paul's Epistle to the Romans as not only a document which eloquently expresses that feeling of disquietude, but as a sacred writing, a communication of the Word of God which sets its seal upon the estimate and declares it not merely to be true but to be the *whole* truth.

Now it must be plain to any impartial observer that the subjective disquietude above referred to varies according to the circumstances of the individual. I do not mean that there is not such a thing as a foolish excess of optimism which is almost invariably followed by a disaster (pride, going before a fall), but that there are plainly, both in individuals and in groups, varying proportions between optimism and disquietude, just as there are varying proportions between health and sickness.

The description of human life as being *to a great extent* "nasty, mean, brutish and short," may be true enough, but it does not necessarily (apart from the

[1] It should be noted that there is an important difference here between Lutheran and Catholic theory. The former regards the Fall as a corruption of Nature, needing to be purged away. The latter treats it as a descent from Supernature into Nature, so that by it Man is deprived of the capacity to attain to the full measure of his being. But it ought to be emphasised that even Paul, whom Baron von Hügel once described as "our first great cataclysmic convert" does not speak of "the Fall", but says "all . . . have fallen short".

fact that it is a deliberate hyperbole) involve a descent from original righteousness, but rather the correct observation that a good deal of that life does not progress beyond the point where it is "a fuss in the mud," or reach a stage in which it is noble and beautiful. That it is potentially capable, however, by some means of making such progress, and is therefore not irretrievably ruined but full of the most glorious possibilities, seems a far truer estimate of mankind than to say "mankind is that which has sinned, is sinning, and will sin, and can recognise itself as nothing else than lost and fallen to eternal perdition."[1]

It is clear that there are, and have been, episodes in the life of the individual and of social groups (such, for example, as central Europe in the twentieth century or the Roman Empire in the fifth) when the pathology of the situation has been more evidently felt than the underlying potential capacity for health; and under such conditions the cataclysmic self-revelation of the Epistle to the Romans will seem, as no doubt it did to Augustine and Luther,[2] to be the true verdict upon humanity. But this involves the elevation of one section of human experience into a position where it becomes the norm or standard for the whole; and must prove to be quite as fatal in excluding from religious fellowship those earnest thinkers who cannot subscribe to the dogmatic statement above, as was the easy-going optimism of a Renaissance pope or of an eighteenth-century Anglican, when it included

---

[1] E. Brunner, in *Der Mittler*. Note also Mrs. Rhys David's remark in the *Hibbert Journal* for 1931.

[2] And now again to the Barthians.

within that same fellowship all sorts of good-natured persons, most of whom were entirely lacking in moral earnestness. The conclusion would therefore seem to be that we should keep our heads and avoid exaggerated extremes of anthropological doctrine.

The effect of the personal twice-born influence of Luther is plainly to be seen in the theological thought of the churches which bear his name, and whose representatives show themselves at the present time unquestionably faithful to the sombre view which he originally expounded. According to Luther there is no way up from man to God. One cannot climb up to communion with Him. Human religion is at best a futile occupation. The only road in existence is that from God to man, the way of revelation through the historical Jesus; and between this and the non-Christian religions the difference is not one of degree within a continuous scheme, but between futility and condescension. Echoes of such teaching are to be found in the careful distinction drawn by a modern Scandinavian theologian[1] between ἔρως, which is merely human passion wilfully striving upward (the libido of our modern psychologists), and ἀγάπη, which is divine love stooping to draw men to itself. There is of course a deep and obvious difference between this and the view of Catholic theology, where although the initiative in the process of assimilation to God must come from the side of the eternal, yet our moral endeavours must be genuinely *ours* and must be real and not fictitious responses to the approach made by Deity.

Catholic theology, like Protestant, is unwilling to

[1] Professor Nygren.

break away from the misleading Fall-phraseology
and rationalises the notion of a historical apostasy;
yet it preserves a place in its system for the non-
pathological features in life. It does not confuse
disease with transitoriness, nor does it arbitrarily sever
the world from God in such a way that it is led to
declare that nothing about the divine nature or purpose
can be discovered by scrutinising the world around us.
But for Lutheran orthodox theology which is true-to-
type there can be logically no natural theology. One
can well understand how religious practice based upon
this theory can have no truck with any kind of humanism, and how it must inevitably issue in some form of
Puritanical creed, with a deep distrust of the arts and
sciences as mere examples of the pride of life. Of
course not all Protestantism is anti-humanistic, and
even that which is, is not necessarily logical. Its
abandonment of logic, however, weakens its distinctive
position, and I do not think that it is inappropriate to
draw attention to these matters at a time when an
œcumenical movement is bringing together people of
Protestant and Catholic antecedents in the hope of re-
uniting them in one fellowship. Such reunion cannot
be expected to get very far, unless on so fundamental
a point as this the pre-suppositions of belief have
been carefully examined; for both cannot be right,
though both may be exaggerations of a central truth.
We see then that the extreme sense of human sinfulness
is found in individuals and groups everywhere, and is
due not merely, as might have been supposed, solely

to the acceptance of some particular dogmatic theory, but to the rationalisation of an uneasiness already existing which colours one's general outlook, and which is present as the result of certain psycho-physiological conditions, either in the individual or the community, leading to what has been called the sin-obsession. These two types obviously correspond to what an American pioneer thinker has described as being "once-born" or "twice-born," or as displaying respectively healthy-mindedness and sickness of soul. Yet outlook in this case is not the same as actuality. The truth about man lies somewhere between the two extremes. The fact about the human species is that it combines both types within itself.

What has been called the sin-obsession is (as has been pointed out) entirely absent from the actual teaching of Christ. Evil is not shirked in His teaching, nor is the peril of the three types of moral evil which we have previously indicated any way minimised. A long succession of Christian thinkers (but only those of a certain type) has insisted that man is so far gone from original righteousness, and of his own nature inclined to evil, that therefore human nature in every person born into the world deserved God's wrath and damnation: and again, that the condition of man after the fall of Adam is such that he cannot turn and prepare himself by his own natural strength and good works to faith and calling upon God.[1] The new anthropology, however, while it in no way denies the fact and possibility of the three

[1] It is a distinct query whether this planet can be described *in toto* (as I have seen it described even in quite recent evangelistic literature) as "God's prodigal world": but at any rate man, apart from religion, soon becomes a prodigal.

types of evil which we have described, has for ever disposed of the historicity of any single individual aberration affecting the entire subsequent course of human development. Failures, deviations, and perversions it recognises, but not a Fall. Human nature it regards as full of promise, though of unstable equilibrium, and as possessed of much good raw material, though liable to lapses. It is necessary, therefore, in the face of these indisputable facts to consider in what sense (if in any) the older theological terms such as Grace, Conversion, Justification and Salvation should be re-interpreted, for that they need a radical re-interpretation must be plain to all who have studied the preceding pages.

2. *Grace*

The old conception of Grace was in the main that of divine favour condescendingly bestowed upon the degraded and corrupt human race. It might be a loving favour, but it was still a favour, something which no one could ever have the right to deserve. It is true that in Catholic theology the word sometimes covers other divine operations of a kind more tender and more positive, but fundamentally what we have said stands true, and it is asserted that man cannot merit the first grace of God. Christian thought in these latter times has come to outline a rather different definition of the term, and has removed it from that field in which merit is a subject for discussion. Grace is now held to be the super-personal activity of the Divine Spirit, the activity proper to His whole character of holy and generous self-giving love, and as such a uniform, unchanging, and unfailing condition of activity. Man as the product and object of this divine activity is held to be entitled to expect the aid and stimulus of that divine personal activity in all his desires, counsels, and works, so long as they are holy, just, and good, but he cannot unconditionally demand it; it is a gift, not a right, and as such he must seek it and qualify for it. In his freedom he may of course choose to live a little narrow life of his own, but even so his continued existence is inevitably dependent upon the unchanging goodwill and ever-ready resources of his Creator.

If, however, he cares to take advantage of it, there is always waiting for him, ready, accessible, and available, not simply the material wealth but the personal friendship of the Divine Spirit, of the Wider Self in co-operation with Whom he can achieve his true self-realisation, and most worthily perform the duties of his station. In isolation and aloofness from this Wider Self he will not necessarily be corrupt and evil (though under such circumstances he is more likely to be so), but he will definitely remain on a lower level, less than he might be and not the best that he might be.

There is a further difference between the old and the new account of what is meant by Grace. The older account tended to detach the action of the Divine Personality from the Personality itself, in such a way as to de-personalise the whole idea of grace and to make it rather of the nature of an impersonal force such as electricity, or of a curative medicine like a tonic in a bottle. The new idea utterly declines to separate grace from personality and insists that wherever the Divine influence is felt there is immediate and direct contact with the Divine Person. There is no "higher gift than grace."

The tendency of the last decade in many circles has been to revert for no conservative reason to a pessimistic view of human nature. It has been said that the new psychology has but few generous illusions regarding it. "This psychology could dot the i's and cross the t's of St. Augustine. It regards human nature as having its roots not merely in the soil but in the dunghill."[1] This is a phase which may easily pass, and upon which, therefore, too much stress need not be laid. It is, however, true that a fairly large section of society has come once again to look for rescue from its animal ancestry less to information derived from the school than to a process of psychic purification. It seeks redemption rather than instruction, or else gives up all hope or expectation of the former and reverts to its wallowing in the mire of vice, declaring that there is nothing in prospect for man except the life of an unpleasant animal. It might be thought that instruction would enable man to break himself of this habit of sinking into a more or less brutish complacency, but such does not seem to be the case. It has been observed that the development of a widespread belief in the power of man to insure for himself an inevitable earthly beatitude coincides usually with a period of moral stagnation or decadence, while, on the other hand, human beings who are really advancing tend to believe less in themselves and more in a Wider Self from whom the saving experiences come, and to show much less self-consciousness and

[1] J. C. Hardwick, *Modern Churchman*.

self-sufficiency. It would be both foolish and superficial to ignore the existence of the tragic element in human life. The idea of the possibility of finding one's true life in union with the Wider Self is either a piece of fantasy-thinking by which we attempt to console our- selves and to effect compensation for the miseries of life, or else it represents something which is true. The words of a modern observer may be read and pondered upon: "Only the sheltered and the shallow can deny the tragedy of life, and any philosophy of religion based on the obscuring of it is merely pleasantry. The attempt to believe in man without believing in God seems to some of us laudable, but we are finding out that it is vain. Belief in man as our deity, loudly proclaimed by the positivist as a simple and rational faith, seems an exploit of the boldest credulity. We can believe much, but not that. The pessimisms of Schopenhauer and St. Augustine are but twin ways of emphasising the incompleteness and inadequacy of our race."[1]

We are to think, then, of Grace as the permanent un- changing active personal relationship of Deity towards the finite nuclei of consciousness which He has brought into being. It is an attitude of permanent goodwill. It is also an attitude of desire that these finite beings shall co-operate with Him harmoniously in the achieve- ment of the eternal purpose. To be aware of this and to be caught up into the larger life even for a brief moment is to feel the effect of grace. Such perception is not automatic or spontaneous in all cases. Most of us live without being aware of the active goodwill of

[1] J. C. Hardwick, *op. cit.*

our Wise Parent, which surrounds us like the air we breathe. Our consciousness of it needs to be awakened, and in special instances its effects upon us need to be pointed out. Fortunately it happens that once they have really been perceived they are not afterwards so easily overlooked. One grows into the habit of looking for them, and daily life becomes interpreted in a new way.

Much ink has been expended upon the problem as to whether an act of free-will precedes or follows Divine Grace. Discussions of this kind irritate the laity and seem to them to be surrounded with an unreal atmosphere. To our forefathers this was not the case, because their picture of man's condition was entirely Augustinian and based upon the firm belief in one great catastrophic fall, which had involved him in ruin out of which he needed rescue. To them he was as it were in a pit from which he was unable to extricate himself. In answer to his call for help there came to him Divine Grace, like a rope thrown to him. His first effective voluntary act in extricating himself was to lay hold of the rope. Thereafter his emergence from the pit became a process of voluntary scrambling up the side of it, holding on to the rope which was pulling him all the time. This picture will not do to-day. We must rather imagine mankind as on the march over difficult country, engaged in a sort of Pilgrims' Progress, not always, but certainly at intervals stumbling, and sometimes even straying out of the right way for long periods. In the midst of the band of pilgrims is the Guide, whose personal help is ever available to all, and whose goodwill to all is constant and unchanging. The details of this new picture must not of course be pressed, but it is in the main a true one and the certainty that the Guide is there from the first, before the pilgrims even assemble, does make Grace come before Free-will. Since, however, the influence and help of the Guide are incapable of being forced upon any individual pilgrim (for violence is not an attribute of Deity) it is obvious that, from the moment he becomes self-conscious and self-determining, the free-will of the individual pilgrim co-exists alongside of the goodwill of the guide. We cannot say with Aquinas that the first voluntary act is not really voluntary because it proceeds from prevenient grace. We say that even if the first voluntary act be the impulse to ask for Divine assistance and inspiration it would still be an autonomous impulse. It would be true enough that that autonomy had once been called into existence by the Divine Spirit himself; but some point there must have been at which Divine Control came to an end and passed over into human freedom.[1]

It is in the light of the foregoing consideration that we have to re-interpret the old theological terms of conversion, justification, salvation, sanctification, inspiration and redemption. As formerly used they were sometimes interchangeable, though of course not in every case, but were on the whole credited with far too clear-cut a meaning. We shall be wiser than our forbears, if we regard them as attempts to describe types of experience, of contact and harmony with the constant and unchanging Wider Self from whom all uplifting and enriching experiences come.

[1] This doctrine of response and co-operation is termed Synergism, and it avoids the over-emphasis upon divine power which is typical of Augustine, and that upon human freedom which is the feature of those who follow his opponent, Pelagius.

3. Conversion

Conversion is not exclusively a religious pheno-menon.[1] It is the unification of the personality, and may be religious or contra-religious; but since religion is concerned with the organisation of life, and its direction upon an ideal end, it is better to say that conversion is always religious, but that it may take diverse and even anti-theistic forms. It is no simple process. Fluctuations may occur throughout the greater part of a lifetime, and unification is sometimes succeeded by lapses and backsliding. Some, connected with re-vivals, are merely superficial and of short duration. It is well to distinguish between (1) conversion proper, which is an individual mutation of progressive value, and which may be either fulminant, *i.e.* sudden, or progressive, *i.e.* extending over a considerable period, (2) counter-conversion, (3) recognition, (4) return, (5) development, and (6) crises of conscience. According to the American psychologists, conversion is a natural phenomenon of adolescence and occurs broadly between the ages of eleven and twenty-five. But this is too severe a restriction of the field, since conversion, though certainly natural, is a complex and gradual psychic process which is prepared by individual conditions over a long period. It is much more than the moral and religious crisis of adolescence. The latter is only an extrinsic or indirect cause, a provocative stimulus which produces effects only in certain individuals. It may happen, therefore, that the completion of

[1] Reference may here be made to Sancte de Sanctis' *Religious Conversion* in the International Library of Psychology, and to Underwood's *Conversion, Christian and non-Christian.*

the process is reached long after adolescence, and even in late middle life. The process, like mutations in biology, presents a longer or shorter period of adjustment or adaptation, during which the individual oscillates. In the end, however, provided that the subject accepts the mutation with his will (either quickly or after a period of conflict) he ends by gaining a new stability of mind and a new condition of equipoise. Conversion being, therefore, a natural, even though not a normal or inevitable experience, may to some extent be predicted as to its form and accidents; but it is not automatic, since the subject must acquiesce in the process.

In other words, the act of volition is the most essential factor in conversion. Prediction must therefore be relative, since, although "every volition must have a substance which it kindles," the psychologist, nevertheless, is always dealing with the behaviour of creatures which are not pure machines, although by an abstract process the mechanical element in them may be emphasised. Psychological prediction is limited by the interference of the unpredictable.

Regarded purely from a theistic standpoint, conversion is the response (quick or gradual) to the atmosphere of grace wherewith we are surrounded. It is the reaction of the soul to its spiritual environment.

It may as well be pointed out here that conversion does not necessarily involve a sense of sin, but often mainly a feeling of satisfaction at having found at once one's vocation and a true interpretation of life. It has been observed that Buddhists in Ceylon who were converted to Christianity described their experience as one of satisfaction at having found (as it seemed to them) that the theistic explanation of the universe was superior to that which they had previously held.   A Buddhist is recorded as having been converted in a few hours by the mere reading of St. Matthew's Gospel, chapters 5 to 9.   He experienced no sense of sin, but it is said that his Buddhism simply fell away from him, as he absorbed the positive religious and ethical teaching of those chapters.

CONCLUSION

We hope we have now said enough (1) to establish the legitimacy and importance of intuitive experience, whether of the milder or intenser kind, as evidence for the nature and activity of Deity; (2) to show that it is capable of being submitted to various tests.

There yet remains, however, the undeniable shrinkage in the extent of the milder kind of intuitive experience, quite apart from any deliberate organised efforts to extirpate it.   It really does not grow in people as readily as it used to do.   This may be partly due to changes in education, and to the inevitable sense of unsettlement and instability accompanying those changes: but it is also largely due to the alteration in actual habits and social customs produced by the development of new types of social organisation in urban and rural areas, and to increased transport facilities.   It has been said that the settled European world is once again taking to nomadism, and that nomads are never creative nor reflective: they only observe and destroy; hence they have little or no

personal religion or developed culture.[1] It would be
hard to find a milieu more hostile to the growth of
reflective religion, noble art, or wise ethics than the
noisy and hideous mechanised civilisation of a modern
town and its environs. A generation of human beings
which has developed an obsession about cutting trees
and destroying hedges, and has invented the modern
arterial road; which gives unlimited licence to adver-
tisers and builders, and cannot recognise as such the
ugliness which it is spreading everywhere—such a
generation is singularly unqualified to make pronounce-
ments about the truth or beauty of religious experience.
If it says that it prefers a football match with a brass
band to a communion service as a suitable occupation
for Christmas morning, it is only condemning itself
out of its own mouth. It has lost—or never found—
one of the deepest treasures of life; and is thereby so
much the poorer and meaner. Those who have fos-
tered the conditions[2] under which such a race of beings
has been able to develop have much to answer for.

Lest anyone should suppose, however, that I desire
to convert all the average individuals of which the
public is made up into pale shadows of Ruysbroeck or
Boehme, let me conclude this chapter by expressing
my full agreement with Richard Baxter when he says:
"Religion is delight in God; this delight, however, is
not the immediate intuition such as the blessed have
in Heaven, nor is it enthusiastick delight consisting

---

[1] Keyserling, *The Recovery of Truth*.

[2] Mr. and Mrs. Hammond (in *The Age of the Chartists*) allege that
the mishandling of the peasant populations in the period of the
Industrial Revolution is responsible for having largely killed their
sense of beauty.

in irrational raptures, nor is it inconsistent with sorrow
and fear when they are duties: but it is the solid
rational complacency of the soul in God and Holiness,
arising from the apprehensions of that in Him which
is justly delectable to us."[1]

I would also add that I do not necessarily include all
wanderers under the condemnation of nomads. Slow
and contemplative progress through natural surroundings may lead to deep religious experience and
communion. But swift and restless transference of
people from place to place and from entertainment to
entertainment, especially on the few occasions when
they would naturally have leisure for thought, can
only tend to generate shallowness and emptiness of
mind.

A few concluding remarks may be offered at this
stage upon the two great lines of approach, the inferential and the intuitive, which we have now in
considerable detail surveyed:—(a) we have seen that
God as a certainty cannot be found as the end of a
syllogism, though as a probability He may be inferred
from it, and a probability may fairly be matter for an
experiment; (b) yet if an experiment can end in an
experience, that experience ought not to prove contrary to logic; (c) it can hardly be called improper
to combine an enlargement and revision of the
teleological and other arguments with the experience
of the prophets and mystics. The latter (as has been
well said) decline to regard their interpretations of
the world as wholly mistaken and misleading, or their

[1] In his *Christian Directory*.

prayers as mere "spiritual dumb-bell exercises."[1]
They claim touch with a real Element which is not
themselves, and though in describing their experiences
they often employ language which imports into those
experiences details belonging to their own special
world of theological and mythological notions,[2] that
language does not empty their experiences of meaning
such as is coherent with logic and science.

It is probably true that science by itself produces
only disbelief, or, rather, bare neutrality without any
indication as to meaning. But no human being can
be content with that.

OF BEHAVIOURISM

In a volume which professes to deal with the psychological aspects of religion, and with the validity of religious
experience, it will naturally be expected that something
should be said about the views of the behaviourist school,
which are considered to be most hostile towards religion.

Behaviourism holds that the characteristic of being a
mind or being a mental process reduces to the fact that a
certain kind of body is making certain overt movements
or is undergoing certain physical changes. As a matter
of fact we can safely leave the refutation of this theory
in the hands of no more orthodox a critic than Prof.
Broad.[3] It is not necessary to profess Christianity or

[1] Inge, on various occasions.

[2] A friend has suggested a comparison between these mythological
notions and the fantasy of Santa Claus. The experience of the
child that on Christmas Eve toys somehow get inside a stocking
is not dependent upon the myth of Santa Claus, but upon the
reality of the benevolent parent who puts the toys where they are
found. The toys do not automatically arrange themselves, and yet
Santa Claus is not a very accurate picture of the benevolent parent.

[3] Tarner Lectures, final chapter, "The Mind and its place in
nature."

even any other religion in order to show that it stands condemned.

According to Broad, behaviourism in psychology is much the same as mechanism in biology. But there is an important difference between the problems of life and of mind, which makes behaviourism less defensible even than mechanism. "The one and only kind of evidence that we can have for believing that a thing is alive is that it behaves in certain characteristic ways such as eating, drinking, digestion, and so on. All these are merely actions of one body upon other bodies and there seems no reason for supposing that 'being alive' means any more than exhibiting such types of behaviour. Hence the controversy about life is really between emergence and mechanism. But the position about consciousness seems to be essentially different, for although part of our evidence for supposing that anything outside ourselves has a mind is that it performs certain bodily movements in certain situations, yet our observation of such behaviour is not our only or even our primary ground for asserting the. existence of mind and mental processes. For in the first place we can distinguish in one of our own mental experiences between that experience and any bodily behaviour which may happen to coincide with it. The two are plainly not of necessity inter-connected. And in the second place there is always a distinction to be drawn between automatic and purposive behaviour. The question 'Has so and so got a mind?' is never meaningless, and never a real synonym for asking 'How does a certain body behave under certain stimuli?' If the behaviourist asserts that it ought to be such a synonym, we are quite justified in saying that in our own case we know the two questions could not be synonymous, and further that, if we are mistaken, it is up to the behaviourist to show how it was possible for us to make the mistake, if, as he says, we are incapable of observing more than bodily behaviour in ourselves and in others.   For if behaviourism be true, then we are all making a mistake of which it would be impossible for us even to think, unless behaviourism was false."

And so we are landed in an absurdity.

But further, Broad goes on to demonstrate that it is exceedingly doubtful whether we can find any kind of molar bodily behaviour which always takes place when a person would be said to be perceiving a certain object, and which never takes place when he would be said not to be perceiving it.   And he concludes that unless this can be found, the attempt to *reduce* perception to some kind of molar bodily behaviour which has some special reference to the perceived object fails at once.   Yet even supposing that by careful investigation such behaviour could be disclosed, Broad insists that there is always something involved in the statement "A is perceiving X" which is over and above the behaviour of A's body in a certain way.   "A's awareness of X" and "a certain behaviour of A's body" are according to the behaviourist just two names for the same characteristic.   But a mental awareness and a molecular movement, though they may be two different but associated characteristics of related objects, cannot be reasonably described as the same characteristic.

I end where I began, with the affirmation that to allow the decay of the deep consciousness of the Greatest of Realities is to acquiesce in the impoverishment of human life.   It resembles in futility an attempt to operate a machine with the electric current which drives it either blocked or cut off.   Conversely, the

acceptance, and the patient and persevering development of that consciousness, lead surely to the constructive enrichment of life.

Very early in my own career I had to make a big
decision.   The exact nature of it I may not reveal to the
public, nor does it matter for the purpose of argument:
suffice it to say that it was as basic in actual life as
that episode in Wellsian fiction, in which the author
represents the poor little cockney, Mr. Polly, as deciding,
after wrestling with his own infirmity, "to go back to the
Potwell Inn", although, as he says, it "ain't no business
of mine".

All I can add is that the decision I made determined
almost the whole course of my subsequent life, that it
must have seemed superficially to many observers to be
limiting and frustrating my activities, and even at times
threatening me with disaster.   Yet in making that
decision I have always felt since then, just as I did at the
time, that unworthy as I certainly was (indeed very
much of an "earthen vessel"), the Power behind and
within phenomena was guiding and directing and
certainly trying to use me.   And after this long-term
experiment, now nearing its end, I can honestly look
back and say: "I have no regrets.   The decision I
made was the correct one.   It enabled me to be used
precisely in the way that was intended, and so far from
sterilising my life, it has actually ended by making it
more constructive than without that decision it could
possibly have become."

And so I would like to conclude by quoting from the
first Spiritual Exercise proposed for meditation by
St. Ignatius Loyola, the founder of the Jesuit Order:

"Man was created to praise, do reverence to, and serve God Our Lord. And other things on the face of the earth were created for man's sake and to help him in the following out of the end for which he was created . . . Wherefore it is necessary to make ourselves detached in regard of all created things—in all that is left to the liberty of our free will . . . so that we on our part should not wish for health rather than sickness, for riches rather than for poverty, for honour rather than ignominy, for a long life rather than a short life, and so in all matters, solely desiring and choosing those things which may better lead us to the end for which we were created."

Fr. Rickaby, commenting on these words, in his edition of the Spiritual Exercises, says that he once gave the passage in retreat to a young sailor boy at a port overseas, and left him alone to meditate. When he returned he found the lad in a great state of excitement, and asked him what he had been doing. "Well, father," replied the boy, "I just walked up and down saying: Damn it, it's true; Damn it, its' true." "My son," said Rickaby, "you have made exactly the right act of meditation."

ADDITIONAL FOOTNOTES

A. Some few years ago Arthur Koestler wrote describing the Japanese people as the most irreligious nation he knew. Today Japan is seething with religious creativity, and its Ministry of Education has registered as many as 171 new religious movements.

B. Mescalin is a drug derived from a root known as peyote, which is used by some tribes of American Indians to induce ecstatic states of consciousness. It was tried by the late Mr. Aldous Huxley, who seems to have approved of its effects; but Professor R. C. Zaehner of Oxford, who has also experimented with it, has taken a less favourable view, and has written a somewhat scathing criticism of Huxley's conclusions, in his book *Mysticism Sacred and Profane*. In view of Zachner's work, it is hard to see how Mr. Christopher Mayhew's letter to *The Times* in July 1967 can be treated seriously, as in challenging the uniqueness of Christian mystical experience he seems to ignore the whole of Zaehner's very careful, learned and responsible work. In speaking of a new drug, L.S.D., for which similar results to mescalin are claimed, Dr. Gough, a psychiatrist at Windsor Hospital, who is also a Christian, has stated publicly that she has had personal experiences of it, and finds no advantage in its alleged stimulus to mystical experience over what can be obtained with one's full senses, by practising normal religious meditation.

The employment of a drug to induce religious exaltation is of course very ancient. A form of sacred alcohol, now apparently obsolete, was used in Vedic India, where it was called *soma*, and in Iran, where it was called *haoma*. Some Indian yogis and some Muslim devotees may use hashish, but yoga in respectable circles seems to be now a matter of physical exercises (hatha yoga) involving breathing control, and other forms of bodily concentration. Actually, as Baudelaire recognised, all that drugs can do is to stimulate artificially whatever capacity a man may possess already. They can bring him nothing new. They are dangerous adventitious aids, leading to evil side-effects, and should be avoided by all, and especially the young.

C. This seems the right moment to point out that much religion, so far from being opium, is intensely stimulating, and drives the believer to acts of sacrifice, self-denial, heroism, and unexpected enterprise which are by no means the fruits of the administration of a narcotic, and offer no pie in the sky, but only the satisfaction of following an ideal which offers no material reward.

D. Provided that one accepts the tripartite classification previously given (see Introduction, page 6).

139

E. Since writing this I have become acquainted with a person who, with an I.Q. in the nineties and with an advanced liberal and modernist interpretation of the Christian faith, still finds it reasonable to speak of "talking to God", and of listening for guidance with humble intimacy.

F. At any rate in Barth's earlier phase.

G. This passage of course refers primarily to the situation as it was in 1932, but the position in 1967 is even more striking, with the foundation of Churchill College, and the immense proliferation of science departments.   In the midst of this, it is worth recording that the Cambridge Divinity Faculty is by some regarded as stronger in its personnel and reputation than it has ever been.

H. This is in effect not very different from what Dr. Billy Graham has done up till recently (although I gather that even he is now slightly and with great caution modifying his statements), namely treating the Christian scriptures magically, and shouting "The Bible says", without considering the propriety of dealing with it uncritically as a verbally inerrant bundle of proof-texts.

I. But such an experiment must needs be a long-term one, and not one hastily or petulantly relinquished after a short trial.

J. It is quite justifiable to work for the total banishment of the exploitation of individuals by one another, or of one class by another. But to do so still leaves unanswered the basic question: "What is the purpose of man's life?"

K. The word for sin (*hamartia*) in the three synoptic Gospels is represented as being used only once by Jesus, whereas in the Epistles it occurs 63 times, 38 of them in the Pauline writings.

L. This is the point made recently by Fr. Charles Davis, i.e. that Divine Grace is available to all human beings, non-Christian and Christian alike.

M. It is unnatural for human beings to live in such vast conurbations that they grow up in a state of unfamiliarity with natural beauty and wild life.   Mankind is not meant to be the predominant or exclusive form of organic life upon the planet.   He needs wildernesses to retire to at intervals, and has a duty to respect and care for the non-human creatures with which he is surrounded.